PASSAGE TO ESL LITERACY

Student Workbook developing skills in:
Visual Discrimination
Sound Symbol Association
Sight Word Recognition
Reading and Writing

Diane M. Longfield
ESL Instructor
ESL Consultant

DELTA SYSTEMS, INC.

1400 Miller Parkway
McHenry, Illinois 60050

Copyright© 1981 by Delta Systems Inc. 1981

ISBN 0-937354-01-5

First published 1981 by
Delta Systems Inc.
6213 Factory Road, Unit B
Crystal Lake, IL 60014

All Rights Reserved. No part of this publication may be reproduced, stored in a retrieval system, or transmitted in any form or by an means, electronic, mechanical, photocopying, recording or otherwise, without the prior permission of the copyright owner.

Printed in the United States of America.

TABLE OF CONTENTS

PART 1 - Pre-Literacy
    Writing Personal Information
    Visual Discrimination

Writing Your Name 1
Numbers 1-10 2
Writing Numbers 1-10 3
Numbers 0-10, Review 4
Writing Your Address 5
Writing Your City and State 6
Writing Your Zip Code 7
Writing Your Telephone Number 8
Writing Your Social Security Number 9
Visual Discrimination: Shapes
    General 10
    Spatial Relations 11
    Directionality 12
Visual Discrimination: letters
    Directionality 13
    Spatial Relations 14
    Vertical, horizontal, diagonal lines 15
    All lines, circles, semi-circles 17
Visual Discrimination: small letters
    Vertical, horizontal, diagonal lines 18
    Vertical lines, circles, semi-circles 19
    Vertical, diagonal lines, semi-circles 20
    Circles, semi-circles, vertical, horizontal
      lines: letters on the writing line 21
    Circles, semi-circles, vertical diagonal
      lines: letters below the writing line 22
Test, Visual Discrimination and Personal Information 23

PART 2 - Literacy 29
    Sound Symbol Association
    Beginning Reading and Writing
    Consonant Blends and Digraphs
    The Alphabet
    Personal Information, continued

Hh, Tt, Ss, Aa, Mm, Nn
    Writing the letters 31
    Visual discrimination/writing words 32
    Reading/writing sentences 33
    Review 34
Bb, Pp, Ll, Ff, Ee, Dd
    Writing the letters 35
    Visual discrimination, words 36
    Reading/writing words 37
    Reading/writing sentences 38
    Review 39

Jj, Gg, Zz, Cc, Kk, Ii
- Writing the letters 40
- Reading/writing sentences 41
- Review 45
- Blends and Digraphs I: sh, sm, gl, fl, sp, sk, ch 46
- Review, Blends and Digraphs I. Sentence Scramble 47

Rr, Oo, Vv, Xx, Ww, Yy, Uu, Qq
- Writing the letters 48
- Visual discrimination/writing 50
- Reading 51
- Writing 52
- Reading signs 53
- Sentence scramble 54
- Blends and Digraphs II: wh, th, st, cl, ph, qu 55
- Review, Blends and Digraphs I, II 57

Extension, Reading signs 58
Test, Sound Symbol Association 59
- Writing the letters 61
- Dictation/personal information 62

Colors 63
- Blends and Digraphs III: bl, gr, sw, br, pl, dr, sn 65
- Reading/Writing 67

Review, Blends and Digraphs I, II, III 68
Blends and Digraphs IV: sl, tr, cr, fr, pr, kn, tw 69
Test, Blends and Digraphs, I, II, III, IV 71
Alphabet: Letter sequence 73
- Capital letters 74
- Small letters 75

Free writing page 76

PART 3 - Reading and Writing correlated to Lessons 1-10 of
Delta's Effective ESL for the 21st Century 77

Lesson One, Section II: What is it? 79
Lesson Two, Section I: What's your address? 85
             Section II: What time is it?
                     It's ___:00/ ___:30. 90
Free Writing Page 98
Lesson Three Section I: What is he/she? 99
             Section II: What's his/her name? 107
Odd Man Out 108
Lesson Four, Section I: What are they? 109
             Section II: Where are you from? 116
Contractions 118
Free Writing Page 120
Lesson Five, Section I: What time is?
                     It's ___ :15/___ :45. 121
             Extension, Where are you from? 127
             Section II: What day is it? 128
Sentence Scramble 132

Test, Lessons One-five and Personal Information 133
Lesson Six,   Section I: How much is it? 137
                Review 141
                Extension 142
                Section II: What's this/that? 144
Lesson Seven, Section I: It's a/an _____ 149
                Section II: What are these/those? 155
Odd Man Out 161
Sentence Scramble 162
Lesson Eight, Section I: He's at the _____. 163
                Section II: He's here/there. 169
Lesson Nine, Section I: Where are they? 175
                Section II: It's a kitchen. 180
Extension: Where do you live? 184
Lesson Ten,   Section I: He's Mr. Lee's son. 185
Test, Lessons Six-Ten and Personal Information 191

PART 4 - Transition to Cursive Writing 195
Cursive 1 letters beginning (↗) 197
Cursive 2 letters beginning (⌒) 200
Cursive 3 letters beginning (⌐) 202
Cursive 4 letters beginning (⌒) 203
Cursive 5 letters beginning (⌐) 204
Cursive 6 letters beginning (∪) 205
Cursive 7 letters beginning (ℐ) 206
Cursive 8 letters beginning (ℓ) 207
Writing a personal letter 208
Test, Cursive writing 209
Free writing pages 211

Part I - Pre-Literacy

Writing Personal Information
Visual Discrimination

Writing Your Name

DIRECTIONS: WRITE YOUR NAME AFTER THE TEACHER WRITES IT.

☺
Name _____
          first   last
name _____
          last   first

Name _____
          first   last
name _____
          last   first

First Name _____
Last Name _____

first name _____
last name _____

Name _____

1.

Numbers 1-10   first name _____

DIRECTIONS: CIRCLE THE CORRECT ANSWER.

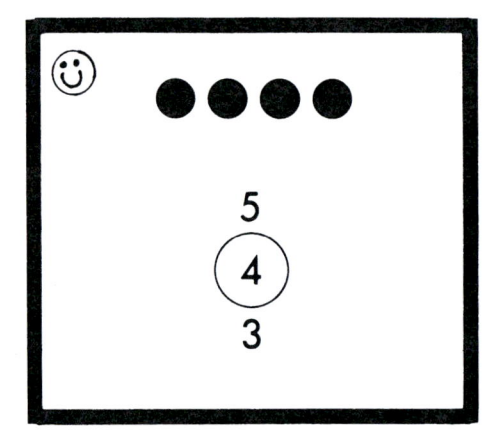

☺ ● ● ● ●
5
(4)
3

1. ● ● ● ● ●
5
7
6

2. ● ● ● ● ●
   ● ● ● ●
10
9
8

3. ● ● ● ●
5
4
3

4. ● ● ● ● ●
   ● ● ●
8
9
7

5. ● ● ● ● ●
   ● ● ● ●
9
10
8

6. ● ● ● ●
   ●
6
7
5

7. ● ●
1
2
3

8. ● ● ● ● ●
   ● ●
7
8
6

9. ● ● ●
2
4
3

2.

Writing Numbers 1-10   last name _____

DIRECTIONS: WRITE THE NUMBERS.

| ●●● 3 | _3_ _3_ _3_ _3_ _3_ |

● 1 ___ ___ ___ ___ ___

●● 2 ___ ___ ___ ___ ___

●●● 3 ___ ___ ___ ___ ___

●●●● 4 ___ ___ ___ ___ ___

●●●●● 5 ___ ___ ___ ___ ___

●●●●●
● 6 ___ ___ ___ ___ ___

●●●●●
●● 7 ___ ___ ___ ___ ___

●●●●●
●●● 8 ___ ___ ___ ___ ___

●●●●●
●●●● 9 ___ ___ ___ ___ ___

●●●●●
●●●●● 10 ___ ___ ___ ___ ___

3.

Numbers 0 - 10, Review

_____
last   first

DIRECTIONS: CIRCLE THE CORRECT ANSWER.

1   ⑤   7   8   6   4

1 2 3 4 5 6 7 8 9 10

1 2 3 4 5 6 7 8 9 10

1 2 3 4 5 6 7 8 9 10

1 2 3 4 5 6 7 8 9 10

1 2 3 4 5 6 7 8 9 10

1 2 3 4 5 6 7 8 9 10

1 2 3 4 5 6 7 8 9 10

1 2 3 4 5 6 7 8 9 10

DIRECTIONS: LISTEN AND WRITE THE NUMBERS.

___ ___ ___ ___ ___ ___ ___ ___ ___ ___

4.

Writing Your Address

_____
Name

DIRECTIONS: WRITE YOUR ADDRESS AFTER THE TEACHER WRITES IT.

☺ Address _____

_____
address

1. Address _____

   address _____

2. _____
   Address

   _____
   address

3. Address _____

   address _____

4. _____
   address

   _____
   Address

Writing Your City and State

Name _____

Address _____

DIRECTIONS: WRITE YOUR CITY AND STATE AFTER THE TEACHER WRITES THEM.

☺ City, State _____
_____
city　　　　　　state

1. City, State _____
city, state _____

2. _____
City　　　　　　State
_____
city　　　　　　state

3. City, State _____
city, state _____

4. _____
City　　　　　　State
_____
city　　　　　　state

6.

Writing Your Zip Code

_____
address

DIRECTIONS: WRITE YOUR ZIP CODE AFTER THE TEACHER WRITES IT.

☺
Zip Code _____
         _____

1. Zip Code _____

   zip code _____

2.
        _____
           Zip Code
        _____
            zip code

3. Zip _____

   zip _____

4. Address _____
           _____

7.

Writing Your Telephone Number

_____
          last   first

DIRECTIONS: WRITE YOUR TELEPHONE NUMBER AFTER THE TEACHER WRITES IT.

☺ Telephone Number _____

_____
telephone number

1. Telephone Number _____

   telephone number _____

2. Telephone _____

   _____
   telephone

3. Phone Number _____

   _____
   phone number

4. Phone No. _____

   _____
   phone no.

5. Home Phone _____

   _____
   home phone

8.

Writing Your Social Security Number

_____
telephone

DIRECTIONS: WRITE YOUR SOCIAL SECURITY NUMBER AFTER THE TEACHER WRITES IT.

☺
Social Security Number _ _ _ – _ _ – _ _ _ _
Social Security Number ☐☐☐ – ☐☐ – ☐☐☐☐

1.
Social Security Number _____ – ___ – _____
              _____ – ___ – _____
              social security number

2.
Social Security Number _ _ _ – _ _ – _ _ _ _
              _ _ _ – _ _ – _ _ _ _
              social security number

3.
Soc. Sec. No.   ☐☐☐ – ☐☐ – ☐☐☐☐
soc. sec. no.   ☐☐☐ – ☐☐ – ☐☐☐☐

4.
Social Security Number _____
              _____
              social security number

Visual Discrimination
General

State _____

Zip Code _____

DIRECTIONS: PUT AN X ON THE SHAPE THAT IS DIFFERENT.

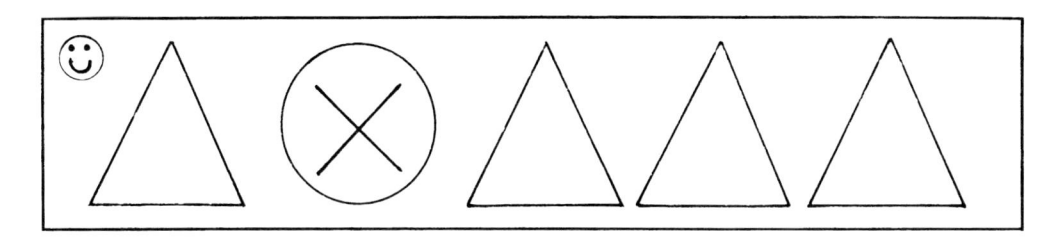

1.

2.

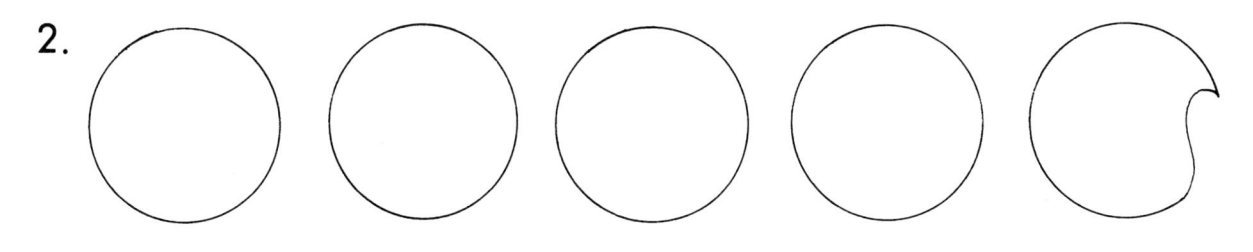

3.

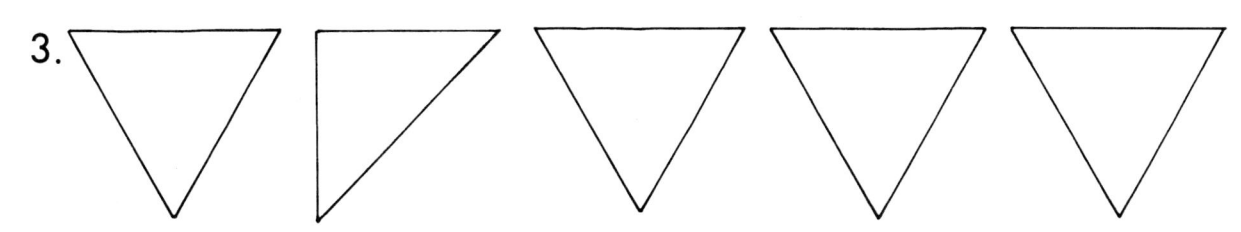

4.

5.

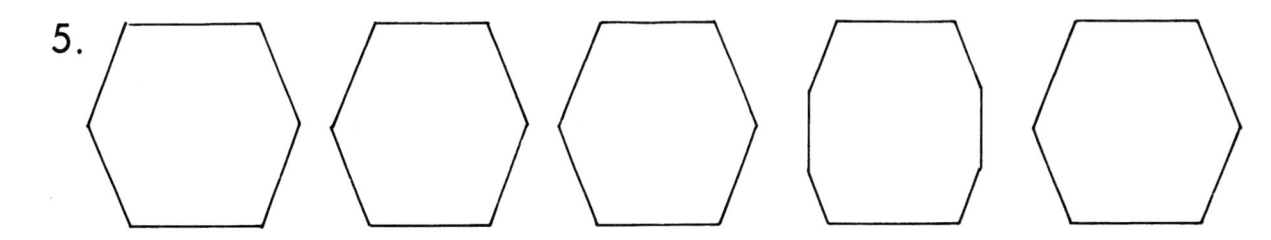

10.

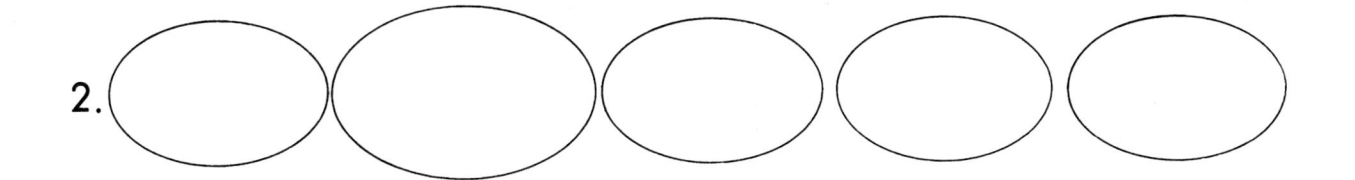

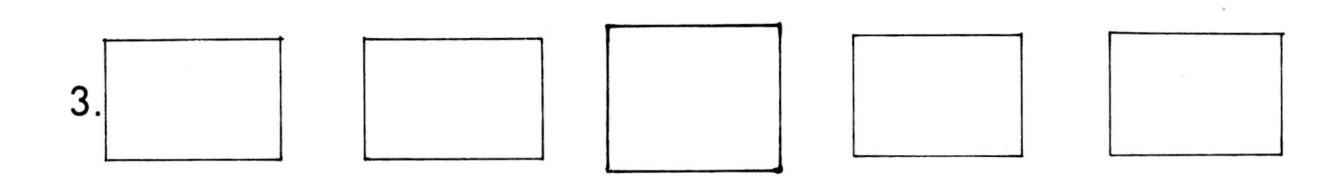

Visual Discrimination
Spatial Relations

city, state _____

zip code _____

DIRECTIONS: PUT AN X IN THE SHAPE THAT IS DIFFERENT IN SIZE.

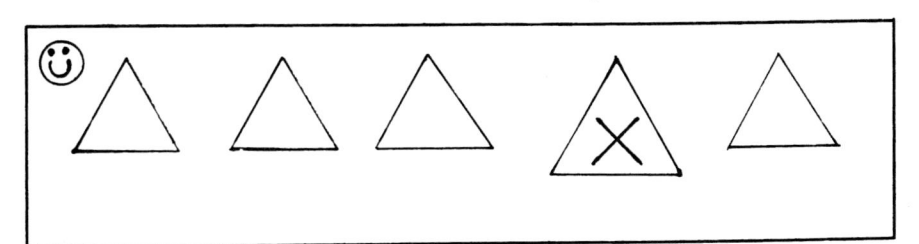

1.

2.

3.

4.

5.

11.

Visual Discrimination
Directionality

Name _____

_____
social security number

DIRECTIONS: PUT AN X ON THE SHAPE THAT IS DIFFERENT.

☺ ⊢   ⊢   ⊢   ⊀   ⊢

1. E   E   Ǝ   E   E

2. Ɔ   C   C   C   C

3. Y   Y   Y   Y   ⅄

4. ⌊   J   J   J   J

5. N   N   N   И   N

6. r   r   r   ⌐   r

7. a   a   a   a   ɒ

8. K   ʞ   K   K   K

9. L   L   L   J   L

10. S   Ƨ   S   S   S

12.

Visual Discrimination
Directionality

_____
city   state

DIRECTIONS: PUT AN X ON THE SHAPE THAT IS DIFFERENT.

☺ b   b   b   ☒   b   b

1. m   m   m   m   m   m

2. q   q   q   q   p   q

3. e   e   e   e   e   ǝ

4. f   ŧ   f   f   f   f

5. h   h   h   h   h   d

6. p   p   q   p   p   p

7. g   g   g   ɓ   g   g

8. ʞ   k   k   k   k   k

9. d   d   b   d   d   d

10. j   j   j   i   j   j

13.

Visual Discrimination
Spatial Relations

Address _____

_____

DIRECTIONS: PUT AN X ON THE LETTER THAT IS DIFFERENT.

| ☺ | p | p | p | p | ✗ |

1. | y | Y | y | y | y |
2. | C | c | c | c | c |
3. | z | z | z | z | Z |
4. | v | V | v | v | v |
5. | P | p | p | p | p |
6. | s | s | s | S | s |
7. | k | k | K | k | k |
8. | o | O | o | o | o |
9. | U | u | U | U | U |
10. | w | w | W | w | w |

14.

Visual Discrimination
Vertical, horizontal, diagonal lines

City ―――――――――
State ―――――――――

DIRECTIONS: CIRCLE THE LETTER THAT IS THE SAME.

☺ L | T   I   E   (L)   H |

1. Z | X   K   Z   Y   A |
2. I | I   L   F   H   T |
3. T | I   L   H   T   F |
4. X | K   Y   Z   A   X |
5. F | I   F   E   T   L |
6. Y | K   X   Z   Y   A |
7. E | F   E   T   I   H |
8. K | X   Z   Y   A   K |
9. H | H   E   I   L   T |
10. A | Y   K   A   Z   X |

15.

Visual Discrimination
Vertical, horizontal, diagonal lines

phone number

DIRECTIONS: CIRCLE THE LETTER THAT IS THE SAME.

☺ Z | X S K (Z) K

1. N | M N V W V
2. Y | V X A V Y
3. M | W N M W V
4. K | K Z X Y Z
5. W | N V M W N
6. X | K X N Y Z
7. V | Y M W N V
8. Z | Z S K Y X
9. A | H F Z A H
10. V | M N V W U

16.

Visual Discrimination
All lines, circles, semi-circles

☐☐☐-☐☐-☐☐☐☐

DIRECTIONS: CIRCLE THE LETTER THAT IS THE SAME.

☺ P | (P)　R　D　B　C

1. B | D　B　R　P　R
2. Q | Q　G　O　J　G
3. D | R　B　D　P　R
4. C | O　Q　G　O　C
5. R | P　B　D　R　P
6. G | Q　C　Q　C　G
7. O | D　O　Q　C　G
8. J | C　G　J　G　Q
9. U | G　J　C　U　C
10. S | Z　S　Z　G　J

Visual Discrimination
Vertical, horizontal, diagonal lines

phone

DIRECTIONS: CIRCLE THE LETTERS THAT ARE THE SAME.

☺   t   f   (t)   k   f   (t)

1. f   k   t   f   f   t

2. k   k   x   f   t   k

3. t   k   t   j   t   f

4. l   i   l   l   h   t

5. w   m   w   n   w   v

6. l   l   h   l   i   t

7. w   w   m   v   w   n

8. i   i   j   l   t   i

9. k   x   k   t   f   k

10. t   x   f   t   t   k

Visual Discrimination
Vertical lines, circles, semi-circles

Name _____
         last   first

zip code _____

DIRECTIONS: CIRCLE THE LETTERS THAT ARE THE SAME.

☺ b | d (b) p q (b) |

1. d | d b d p h |

2. g | g p y g q |

3. h | b h d h f |

4. p | b d p q p |

5. q | p q y g q |

6. d | d b p d h |

7. n | h n r n h |

8. b | b d b p q |

9. p | q p g p h |

10. h | b h d b h |

19.

Visual Discrimination
Vertical and diagonal
lines, semi-circles

address _____

_____
city   state

_____
zip

DIRECTIONS: CIRCLE THE LETTERS THAT ARE THE SAME.

v (v) n r w (v)

1. n | n   u   r   o   n
2. m | r   w   m   n   m
3. f | h   d   f   b   f
4. r | r   n   r   v   i
5. h | b   h   n   r   h
6. m | w   r   n   m   m
7. f | f   k   t   f   t
8. n | n   n   u   h   r
9. r | n   r   r   h   u
10. h | p   r   h   h   n

Visual Discrimination
Circles, semi-circles, vertical
and horizontal lines

soc. sec. number

DIRECTIONS: CIRCLE THE LETTERS THAT ARE THE SAME.

☺ c   o   (c)   e   (c)   u

1. c   c   o   c   e   u

2. e   c   e   e   a   c

3. o   e   o   c   u   o

4. a   a   c   e   a   u

5. u   e   n   a   u   u

6. e   e   c   a   o   e

7. u   n   u   u   a   c

8. c   c   e   a   c   o

9. o   a   o   c   o   e

10. a   o   c   a   u   a

Visual Discrimination
 Circles, semi-circles, vertical
 and diagonal lines

name _____

address _____

DIRECTIONS: CIRCLE THE LETTERS THAT ARE THE SAME.

☺ g | v (g) (g) p q

1. y | g y y j p
2. j | j i g y j
3. g | j g g y q
4. y | y g g y j
5. p | q y h p p
6. j | g j y j i
7. q | p q n j q
8. p | p n p g q
9. g | j q p g g
10. q | q p q g y

Visual Discrimination
Test, p. 1

home phone
_____

DIRECTIONS: CIRCLE ALL THE LETTERS THAT ARE THE SAME.

☺ r   (r)   n   h   (r)   J   i

M   W   V   N   n   (M)   v

1. B | P   B   D   B   F   R
2. v | v   m   n   v   u   w
3. T | F   f   I   T   J   F
4. p | T   p   D   B   p   d
5. Q | Q   C   U   O   G   Q
6. j | j   j   i   I   p   g
7. G | B   C   Q   G   G   C
8. x | K   x   y   K   Z   x
9. q | q   p   q   d   g   g
10. E | E   F   I   T   E   H

23.

Visual Discrimination
Test, p. 2

Name _____

DIRECTIONS: CIRCLE ALL THE LETTERS THAT ARE THE SAME.

☺ r (r) n h (r) u i

M W v N n (M) v

1. H | N H A F T H
2. K | K x K X Z U
3. i | i L T t i j
4. r | j r n h r e
5. Z | Z Z S S Z N
6. m | w m u n w m
7. f | t d f m s f
8. c | c z e c o c
9. S | z S Z t T S
10. L | L I L i F L

24.

Visual Discrimination
Test, p. 3

city   state

DIRECTIONS: CIRCLE ALL THE LETTERS THAT ARE THE SAME.

r | (r) n h (r) u i
M | W N V n (M) v

1. D | P D O D F D
2. w | m n w u w v
3. Y | A V Y J Y F
4. A | H V F A N T
5. g | j g q g p d
6. O | a c C O G O
7. u | y n u v V n
8. F | T D F F T D
9. I | T L I I I I
10. n | m n m o u r

Visual Discrimination
Test, p. 4

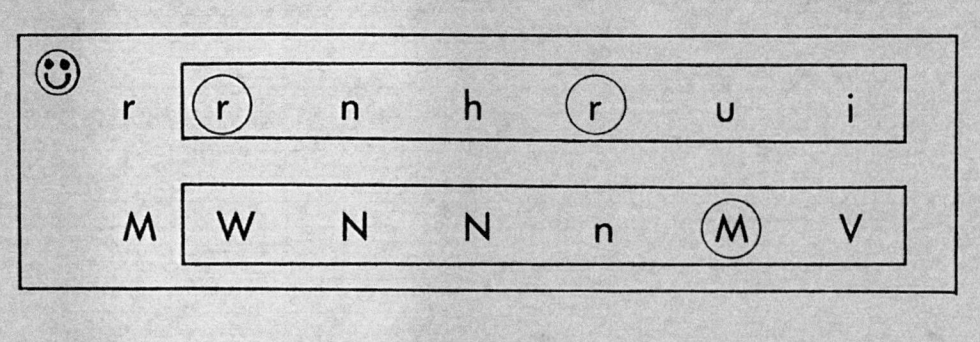

telephone

DIRECTIONS: CIRCLE ALL THE LETTERS THAT ARE THE SAME.

r | r | n | h | r | u | i
M | W | N | N | n | M | V

1. d | b | a | d | g | d | q
2. M | M | W | M | V | N | M
3. y | g | q | y | p | q | y
4. l | i | l | T | I | l | I
5. R | B | R | P | F | b | R
6. k | x | Z | z | X | k | k
7. U | n | V | U | W | v | U
8. z | C | k | z | S | i | z
9. W | V | W | M | v | M | W
10. t | f | t | f | l | F | t
11. a | c | e | u | a | n | o

26.

Visual Discrimination
Test, p. 5

Name

DIRECTIONS: CIRCLE ALL THE LETTERS THAT ARE THE SAME.

☺ r | ⓡ n h ⓡ u i
M | w v N W Ⓜ v

1. V | V u N V W V
2. s | s s Z c s a
3. b | b I b q p P
4. N | M N V m N M
5. e | c a e z e c
6. J | l J g p o d
7. X | Y X K X Z K
8. C | G s a O C C
9. h | r h q p n h
10. P | P d P O R b
11. o | c o n o c C

27.

Personal Information
Test, p. 6

Name _____
          last   first

DIRECTIONS: WRITE YOUR NAME AND ADDRESS.

1.

_____
_____
_____

Ben Lee
109 Fay Ave.
Los Angeles, California
          91107

DIRECTIONS: WRITE.

2.

Identification

Name _____
          last   first
Address _____
_____
          city   state   zip code
Telephone number _____
Social Security Number _____

DIRECTIONS: LISTEN AND WRITE THE NUMBERS.

3. ___ ___ ___ ___ ___ ___ ___ ___ ___ ___ ___

Part 2 - Literacy

**Sound Symbol Association
Beginning Reading and Writing
Consonant Blends and Digraphs
The Alphabet
Personal Information, continued**

Hh, Tt, Ss, Aa, Mm, Nn
Writing The Letters

Social Security No. _____ - __ - ____

DIRECTIONS: WRITE.

1. H
   h

2. T
   t

3. S
   s

4. A
   a

5. M
   m

6. N
   n

Hh, Tt, Ss, Aa, Mm, Nn
Visual discrimination/writing words

Social Security Number

☐☐☐ – ☐☐ – ☐☐☐☐

DIRECTIONS: CIRCLE THE WORD THAT IS THE SAME.

sat | tas   at   mat   (sat)

1.	man	nam	ran	man	nar
2.	hat	tha	bat	hta	hat
3.	Ann	nnA	Ann	An	Auu
4.	at	at	ta	af	cf
5.	has	sha	has	ash	hsa
6.	Sam	Sam	mas	SaM	sam

DIRECTIONS: READ AND WRITE.

hats   hats   hats   hats   hats

1. man
2. hat
3. Ann
4. at
5. has
6. Sam

32.

Hh, Tt, Ss, Aa, Mm, Nn
Reading/Writing Sentences

Name _____

DIRECTIONS: READ AND WRITE THE SENTENCES.

1.  Sam's a man.

2.  Sam has a hat.

3.  Ann has 2 hats.

Hh, Tt, Ss, Aa, Mm, Nn
Review

home phone _____

DIRECTIONS: LISTEN AND CIRCLE THE LETTER THE TEACHER SAYS.

| ☺ | d | b | n | r | (h) |

1. | n | w | m | v | u |
2. | z | b | t | s | o |
3. | d | s | o | u | a |
4. | n | m | u | r | v |
5. | n | h | r | m | b |
6. | t | f | c | h | i |

DIRECTIONS: LISTEN AND WRITE THE SENTENCES.

1. _____

2. _____

3. _____

Bb, Pp, Ll, Ff, Ee, Dd
Writing The Letters

———————————————
Number   Street

DIRECTIONS: Write.

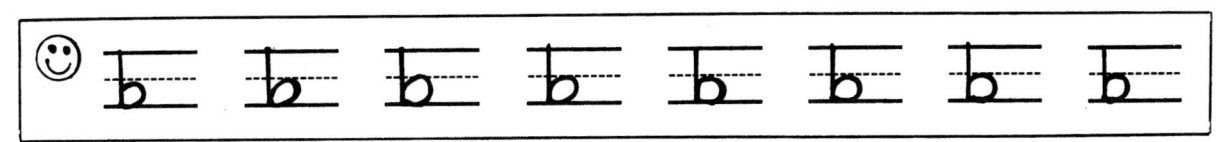

☺ b b b b b b b b

1. B
   b

2. P
   p

3. L
   l

4. F
   f

5. E
   e

6. D
   d

35.

Bb, Pp, Ll, Ff, Ee, Dd
Visual discrimination, words

phone _____

DIRECTIONS: CIRCLE THE WORD THAT IS THE SAME.

☺ bat | fat pat (bat) dat

1. Ben | Pen Ben Ban Bem
2. Lee | Fee eLe Lee tee
3. pen | pen ben pem pne
4. last | lasf last lest tesl
5. name | same mane nane name
6. he | de eh Ban he
7. dad | ded dad dda add
8. fat | fat lat taf fta
9. pet | qet pat pet bet
10. mad | mad nad mab med
11. fast | last tasf fasl fast
12. sad | sab sad sed asd

36.

Bb, Pp, Ll, Ff, Ee, Dd
Reading/writing words

City   State   Zip

DIRECTIONS: READ AND WRITE THE WORDS.

☺ pets   pets   pets   pets

1. Ben Lee

2. pen

3. last name

4. he

5. dad

6. fat

7. pet

8. mad

9. fast

10. sad

Bb, Pp, Ll, Ff, Ee, Dd
Reading/Writing sentences

soc. sec. no.

DIRECTIONS: READ AND WRITE.

Ben's a man.

He has a pen.

Ben's last name's Lee.

Sam's a dad.

He has a fat bat.

He has a fast pet

He's mad.

He's sad.

38.

Bb, Pp, Ll, Ff, Ee, Dd
Review

Address _____

DIRECTIONS: CIRCLE THE CAPITAL AND SMALL LETTER THE TEACHER SAYS.

☺ (M) n (m) o p

1. d b D B q
2. b D B d p
3. f t L T l
4. e a E A d
5. b d p q P
6. m n w M N
7. t F T f t
8. m r n N M

DIRECTIONS: LISTEN AND WRITE THE SENTENCES.

1. _____
2. _____
3. _____
4. _____
5. _____
6. _____

39.

Jj, Gg, Zz, Cc, Kk, Ii
Writing The Letters

home phone

DIRECTIONS: WRITE.

☺ J J J J J J J J

1. J
   j
2. G
   g
3. Z
   z
4. C
   c
5. K
   k
6. I
   i

40.

Jj, Gg, Zz, Cc, Kk, Ii
Reading/Writing Sentences

Age _____

DIRECTIONS: WRITE.

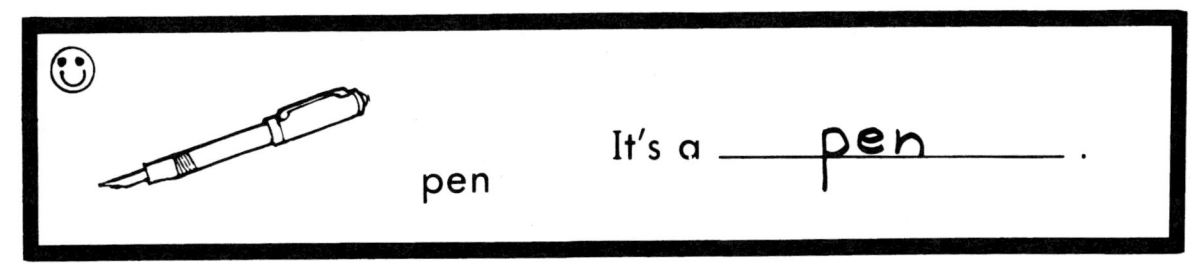

pen — It's a **pen**.

1. flag — It's a _____.
2. lamp — It's a _____.
3. bed — It's _____.
4. cat — _____.
5. jet — _____.
6. hand — _____.

41.

Jj, Gg, Zz, Cc, Kk, Ii,
Reading/Writing Sentences

phone

DIRECTIONS: READ AND WRITE.

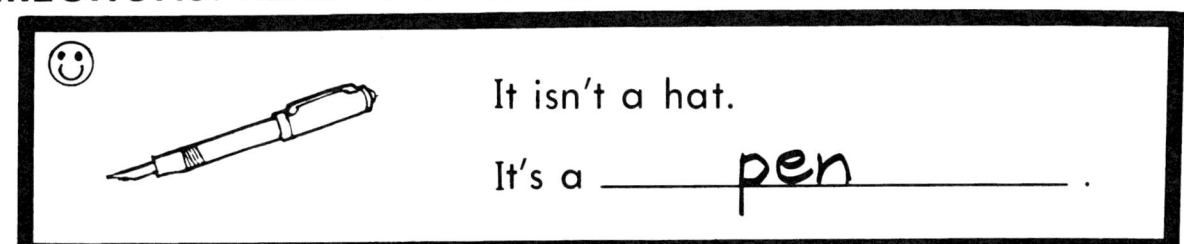

It isn't a hat.
It's a ___pen___.

1. It isn't a cat.
   It's a _____.

2. It isn't a jet.
   It's _____.

3. It _____ flag.
   _____.

4. It _____ hand.
   _____.

5. _____ lamp.
   _____.

6. _____ hat.
   _____.

42.

Reading

zip code

DIRECTIONS: READ.

1.
Sam: Hi, Ken.
Ken: Hi, Sam.
Sam: Is Jan OK?
Ken: She's not well.

2.
She's ill.
She's sick.
She's in bed.

3.
He's not small.
He's tall.

4.
Dad gets a kiss.

5.
She gets gas.

6.
31579

His zip is 31579.

7.
Ben sings.

8.
Sam and Ben sing.

43.

Reading/writing   Age _____

DIRECTIONS: READ AND WRITE.

1. Ben Lee is at the mall. He has a small lamp and tennis balls. Ben's glad.

   Ben Lee _____ mall.
   He _____ small _____ and
   _____ Bens

2. Jan is sick in bed. | She takes a pill. | She's fine.

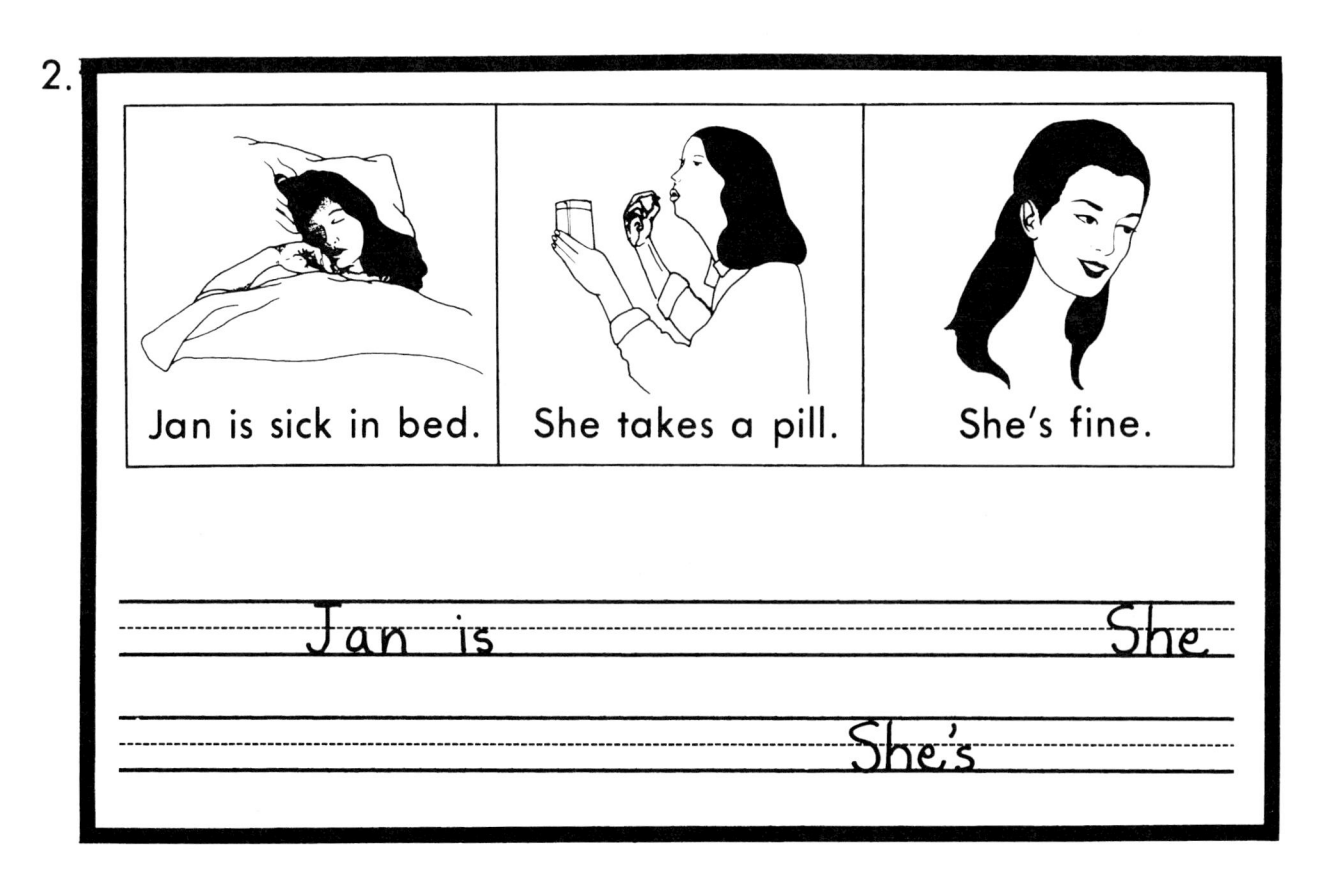

   Jan is _____ She
   _____ She's

Jj, Gg, Zz, Cc, Kk, Ii,
Review

_____
city   state   zip

DIRECTIONS: LISTEN. CIRCLE THE CAPITAL AND SMALL LETTER.

☺   M   (N)   (n)   u   m

1.   f   t   I   T   F
2.   J   i   j   y   Y
3.   z   S   c   s   Z
4.   F   E   a   e   c
5.   x   K   X   k   z
6.   C   j   G   y   g
7.   i   l   T   I   L
8.   i   j   L   j   I
9.   B   d   b   p   D
10.   a   z   z   C   c

DIRECTIONS: LISTEN AND WRITE.

1. Ben Lee is _____ the mall. He _____ a small _____ and tennis _____ . Ben's _____ .

2. Jan is _____ in bed. She takes ___ pill. _____ fine.

Blends and Digraphs I
sh, sm, gl, fl, sp, sk, ch

Mr.
Mrs. _____
Miss
Ms.

DIRECTIONS: READ AND WRITE.

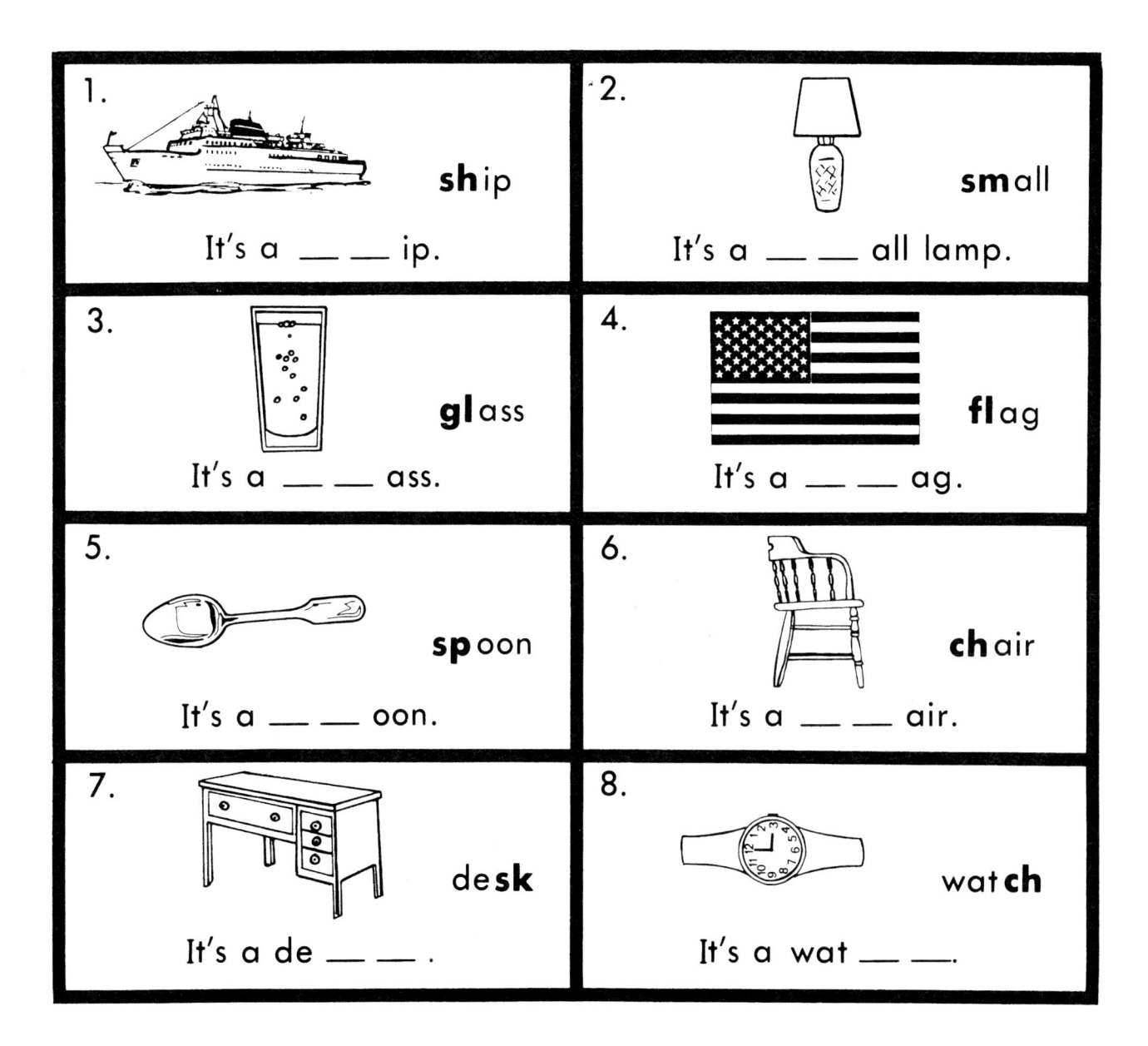

wat **ch**

It's a wat <u>c h</u>.

1. **sh**ip

   It's a __ __ ip.

2. **sm**all

   It's a __ __ all lamp.

3. **gl**ass

   It's a __ __ ass.

4. **fl**ag

   It's a __ __ ag.

5. **sp**oon

   It's a __ __ oon.

6. **ch**air

   It's a __ __ air.

7. de**sk**

   It's a de __ __ .

8. wat**ch**

   It's a wat __ __ .

16.

Blends and Digraphs I
Review

State _____

Zip _____

DIRECTIONS: LISTEN AND WRITE.

1. __ __ ip
2. __ __ all
3. __ __ air
4. de __ __
5. __ __ ag
6. __ __ ass
7. __ __ oon
8. wat __ __

DIRECTIONS: UNSCRAMBLE.

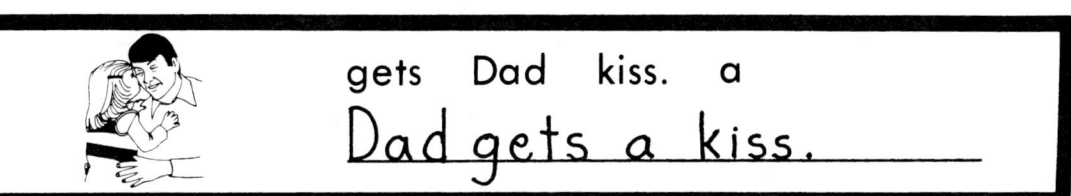

gets Dad kiss. a
Dad gets a kiss.

1. is sick. not Jan
   _____

2. and Ben Sam sing.
   _____

3. glass. It's small a
   _____

4. has Lee balls. Ben tennis
   _____

5. His is 31579. code zip
   _____

47.

Rr, Oo, Vv, Ww, Xx, Yy, Uu, Qq
Writing The Letters

no. street

DIRECTIONS: WRITE THE LETTERS.

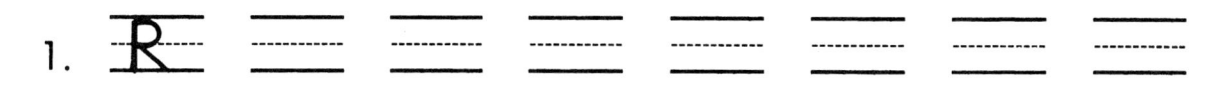

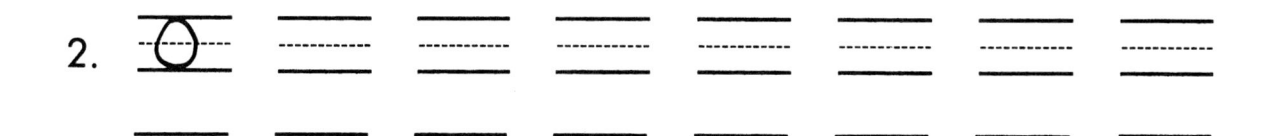

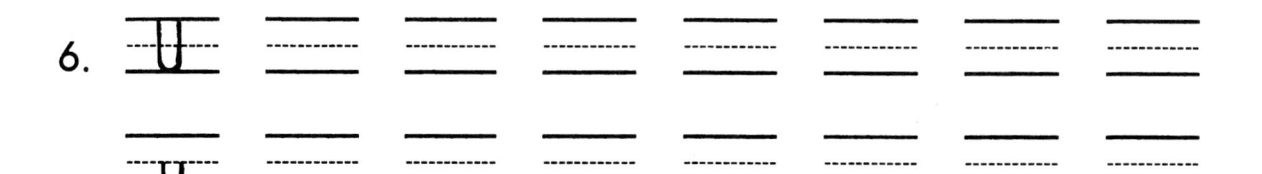

1. R
   r

2. O
   o

3. V
   v

4. W
   w

5. X
   x

6. U
   u

7. Qu

qu

8. Y

y

Rr, Oo, Vv, Ww, Xx, Yy, Uu, Qq
Visual Discrimination/Writing

Mr.
Mrs.
Miss _____
Ms.

DIRECTIONS: CIRCLE THE WORD THAT IS THE SAME.

☺ you | your (you) uou yuo

1.	Hello	Helo	Hell	Hello	Hallo
2.	yes	ues	yse	ges	yes
3.	Thank	Thank	Thak	Thenk	Tank
4.	first	fist	first	frist	frst
5.	your	yuor	you	your	yours
6.	are	rae	are	cre	aer
7.	sex	sex	sxe	scx	sek
8.	how	dow	hwo	box	how
9.	What	Wat	What	Wtah	Whta
10.	you	yuo	your	you	yes

DIRECTIONS: READ AND WRITE.

1. Thank you. _____

2. How are you? _____

3. Hello. _____

30.

Reading Address _____
_____

DIRECTIONS: READ.

1. 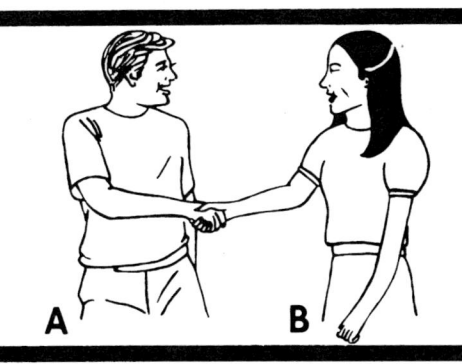
   A: Hi.
   B: Hello.
   A: How are you?
   B: Fine, thank you.

2. 
   A: Hello. How are you?
   B: Fine, thank you.
   A: What's your name?
   B: My name's Ben Lee.
   A: What's your first name?
   B: My first name's Ben.
   A: What's your last name?
   B: My last name's Lee.

3.
My name's Ben Lee.
My first name's _____.
My last name's _____.

4. 
My name's Kay Nelson.
My first name's _____.
My last name's _____.

Writing   phone number _____

DIRECTIONS: WRITE.

1. What's your name?

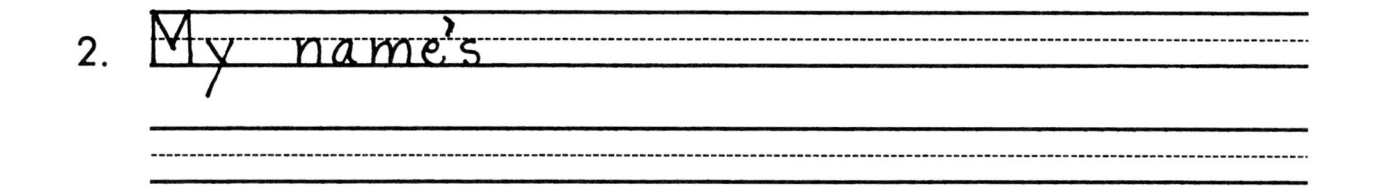

2. My name's

3. What's your first name?

4. My first name's

5. What's your last name?

6. My last name's

Reading signs

Age ☐ 16-20 ☐ 21-35
☐ 36-50 ☐ 51-65
☐ 66-80

DIRECTIONS: READ THE SIGNS.

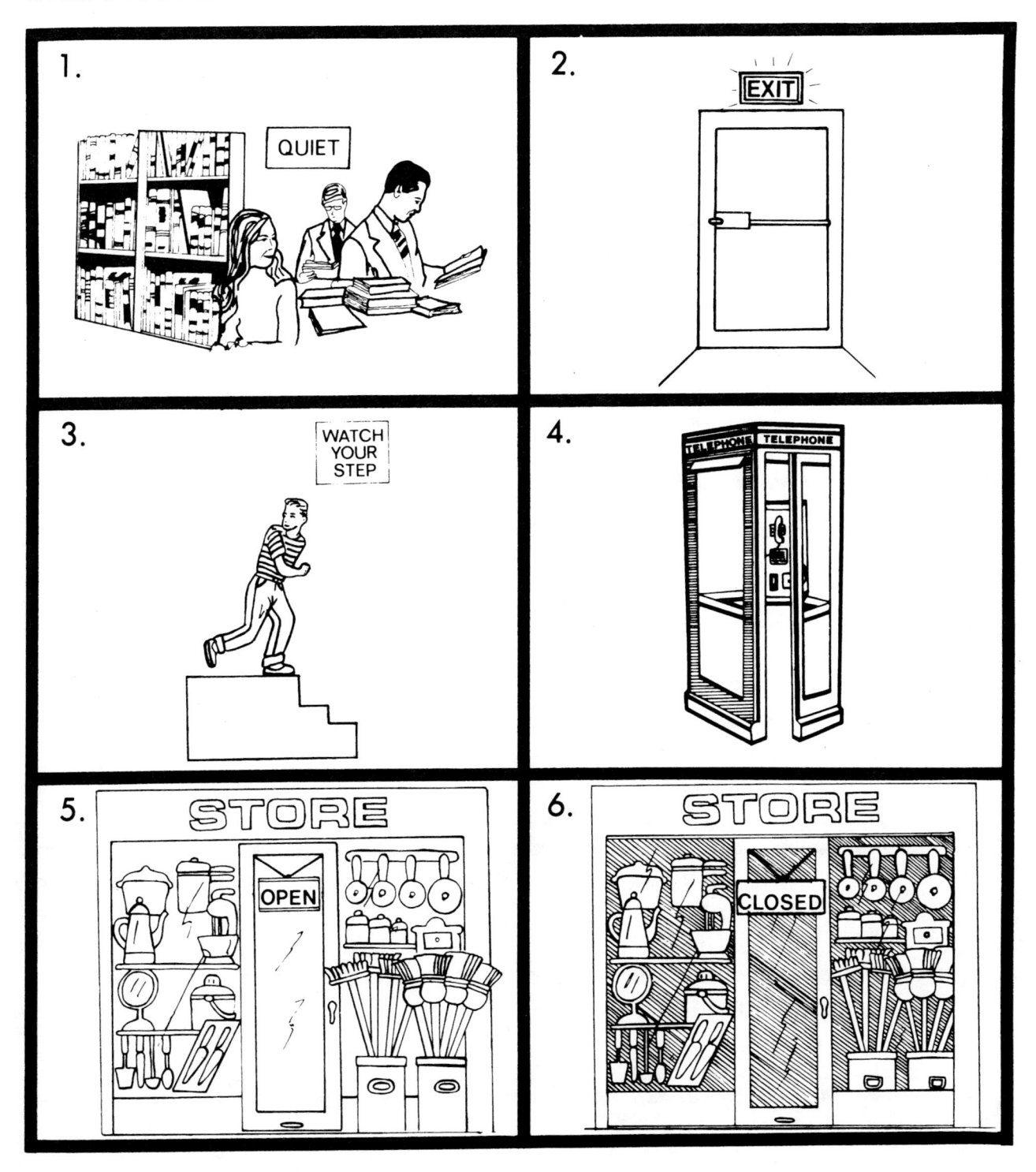

1. QUIET

2. EXIT

3. WATCH YOUR STEP

4. TELEPHONE

5. STORE — OPEN

6. STORE — CLOSED

53.

Phone No.

7. No U Turn

8.

9.

10. CHECK OUT

DIRECTION: UNSCRAMBLE.

1. you? How are
   _____

2. last your What's name?
   _____

3. Nelson. name's Kay My
   _____

4. you. Fine, thank
   _____

54.

Blends and Digraphs II
wh, th, st, cl, ph, qu

☐ Male
☐ Female

DIRECTIONS: READ AND WRITE.

closed

Is it _c_ _l_ osed?
Yes, it's _c_ _l_ osed.

1. **wh**ale

Is it a __ __ ale?
Yes, it's a __ __ ale.

2. **th**ree

Is it a __ __ ree?
Yes, it's a __ __ ree.

3. **st**op

Is it a __ __ op sign?
Yes, it's a __ __ op sign.

4. **qu**arter

Is it a __ __ arter?
Yes, it's a __ __ arter.

5. tele**ph**one

Is it a tele __ __ one?
Yes, it's a tele __ __ one.

6. **cl**ock

Is it a __ __ ock?
Yes, it's a __ __ ock.

55.

Blends and Digraphs II
wh, th, st, cl, ph, qu

___ ___ ___ - ___ ___ - ___ ___ ___ ___

DIRECTIONS: LISTEN AND WRITE.

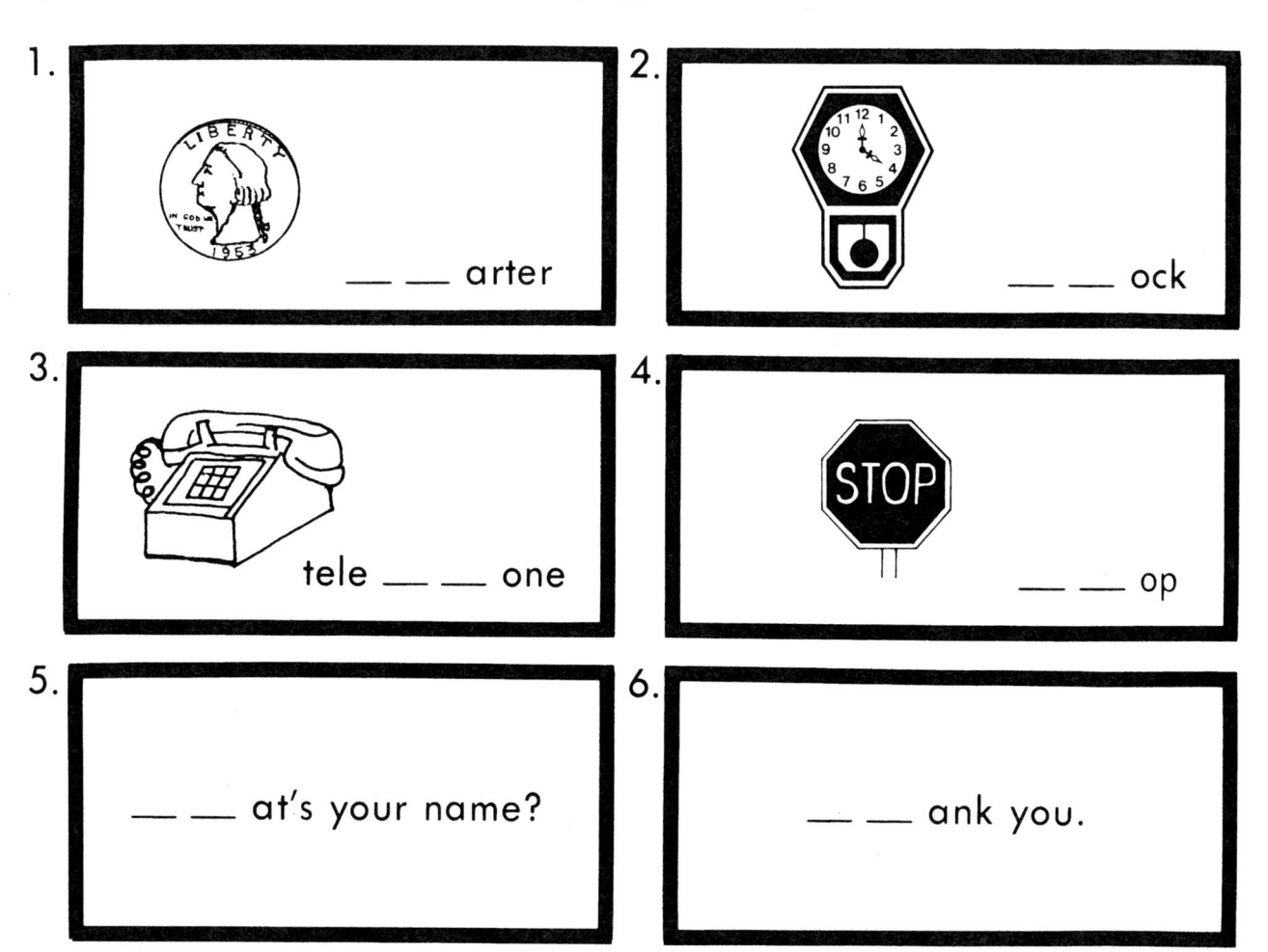

1. __ __ arter

2. __ __ ock

3. tele __ __ one

4. __ __ op

5. __ __ at's your name?

6. __ __ ank you.

DIRECTIONS: LISTEN. UNDERLINE THE SOUND THE TEACHER SAYS.

☺ fir<u>st</u>

1. thank you
2. last
3. what
4. class
5. phone
6. street

7. when
8. thanks
9. state
10. first
11. clock
12. north

56.

Rr, Oo, Vv, Ww, Xx, Yy, Uu, Qq
Blends and Digraphs I, II
Review

☐ Mr.   ☐ Miss
☐ Mrs. ☐ Ms.

DIRECTIONS: LISTEN AND CIRCLE THE LETTER.

| ☺ | p | b | h | t | (v) |

1. | a | e | i | u | o |
2. | r | n | u | h | b |
3. | i | y | q | p | g |
4. | k | z | s | c | x |
5. | a | e | o | i | u |
6. | v | w | m | n | x |
7. | w | n | u | v | b |
8. | j | g | y | i | p |

DIRECTIONS: LISTEN AND WRITE.

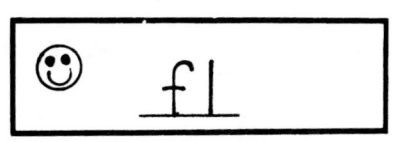

☺ fl

1. ___   5. ___   9. ___
2. ___   6. ___   10. ___
3. ___   7. ___   11. ___
4. ___   8. ___   12. ___

Extension, Reading signs

phone no.

DIRECTIONS: READ THE SIGNS.

1. SPEED LIMIT 45 M.P.H.	2. HILL
3. PUSH	4. PULL
5. CASHIER	6. NO SMOKING
7. RESTROOMS → MEN WOMEN	

58.

Sound Symbol Association
Test, p. 1

name

DIRECTIONS: LISTEN. CIRCLE THE LETTERS.

| ☺ | f | c | b | p | (t) | l | d |

1. b   l   a   i   n   f   p
2. z   s   l   b   i   n   a
3. t   f   z   l   b   n   i
4. c   p   t   f   b   i   n
5. n   i   l   b   f   t   z
6. l   b   n   t   i   a   p
7. s   l   b   i   n   a   l
8. p   t   f   b   i   n   t
9. t   f   b   i   l   a   p
10. x   i   h   k   r   w   qu
11. u   a   n   e   m   v   t
12. qu   r   u   b   v   o   p
13. r   g   h   v   x   i   b

59.

Sound Symbol Association
Test, p. 2

_____
city   state   zip

DIRECTIONS: LISTEN. CIRCLE THE LETTERS.

| ☺ | p | t | f | (b) | i | n | t |

1. g   j   r   v   k   u   w
2. o   d   j   y   u   x   z
3. j   u   i   a   n   e   r
4. qu   y   u   w   k   v   r
5. j   i   n   k   v   r   o
6. g   h   e   n   i   o   b
7. x   s   m   z   c   v   k
8. a   c   u   n   e   g   s
9. qu   x   j   u   w   v   m
10. t   b   p   qu   d   a   h
11. a   w   o   n   qu   d   r
12. f   t   l   x   s   k   e
13. t   d   k   f   l   x   z

60.

Writing the letters
Test, p. 3

_____
telephone

DIRECTIONS: MATCH THE CAPITAL LETTER WITH THE SMALL LETTER.

A	c	H	j	O	q	V	w
B	g	I	l	P	r	W	y
C	a	J	n	Q	o	X	v
D	e	K	h	R	t	Y	z
E	f	L	m	S	p	Z	x
F	b	M	k	T	u		
G	d	N	i	U	s		

DIRECTIONS: LISTEN. WRITE THE LETTER.

CAPITALS

1. I
2. _____
3. _____
4. _____
5. _____
6. _____
7. _____
8. _____
9. _____
10. _____
11. _____
12. _____
13. _____

SMALL

1. m
2. _____
3. _____
4. _____
5. _____
6. _____
7. _____
8. _____
9. _____
10. _____
11. _____
12. _____
13. _____

Dictation/Personal Information
Test, p. 4

Mr.
Mrs.
Miss   _____
Ms.

DIRECTIONS: LISTEN AND WRITE.

1. _____
2. _____
3. _____
4. _____
5. _____
6. _____
7. _____
8. _____

IDENTIFICATION

☐ M
☐ F   Age ____

___ Mr.   ___ Miss
___ Mrs. ___ Ms.   _____
             last   first

Address   _____
          no.   street

          _____
          city   state   zip

_____
home phone   ☐☐☐ – ☐☐ – ☐☐☐☐

Colors

DIRECTIONS: READ.

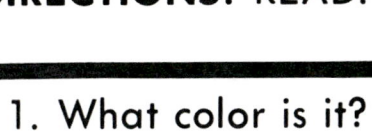

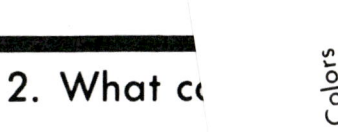

1. What color is it? It's white.	2. What color is it? It's black.
3. What color is it? It's brown.	4. What color is it? It's red.
5. What color is it? It's green.	6. What color is it? It's blue.

DIRECTIONS: CIRCLE THE CORRECT ANSWER.

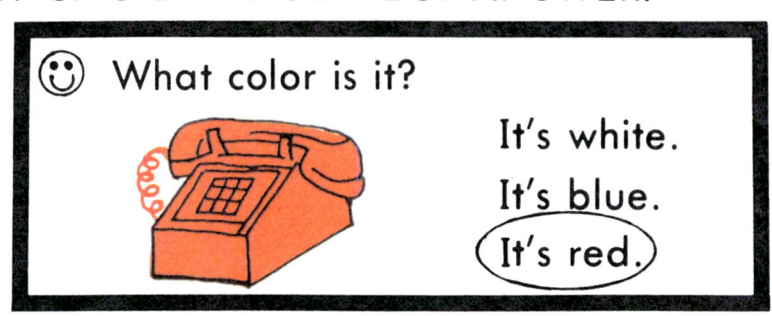

☺ What color is it?

It's white.
It's blue.
(It's red.)

1. What color is it?

   It's brown.
   It's blue.
   It's black.

2. What color is it?

   It's white.
   It's red.
   It's yellow.

3. What color is it?

   It's white.
   It's yellow.
   It's orange.

4. What color is it?

   It's black.
   It's brown.
   It's blue.

5. What color is it?

   It's black.
   It's brown.
   It's gray.

6. What color is it?

   It's green.
   It's gray.
   It's orange.

Colors
Blends and Digraphs III
   bl, gr, sw, br, pl, dr, sn

___ M ___ F

DIRECTIONS: READ AND WRITE.

☺ What is it?

bl

It's a b l ack cat.

1. What is it?

green

It's a ___ ___ een plant.

2. What is it?

sweater

It's a blue ___ ___ eater.

3. What is it?

brown

It's a ___ ___ own desk.

4. What is it?

plant

It's a green ___ ___ ant.

5. What is it?

dress

It's a red ___ ___ ess.

6. What is it?

snowman

It's a white ___ ___ owman.

65.

Colors
Blends and Digraphs III

no.   street

DIRECTIONS: WRITE THE COLOR.   **DIRECTIONS:** WRITE THE WORD.

1. The dress is _____ .   1. The _____ is blue.

2. The plant is _____ .   2. The _____ is brown.

3. The sweater is _____ .   3. The _____ is white.

4. The desk is _____ .   4. The _____ is green.

5. The snowman is _____ .   5. The _____ is black.

6. The cat is _____ .   6. The _____ is red.

Reading/writing

hair color

DIRECTIONS: READ AND WRITE THE COLORS.

1.

The American flag is red, white and blue.
My flag is _____ .

2.

The apple is red and the stem is brown.

3.

Ben has yellow tennis balls.

4.

The stop sign is red and the speed limit sign is black and white.

5.

My home phone is _____ .

6.

My hair is _____ and my eyes are _____

67.

Review
Blends and Digraphs I, II, III

eye color: _____

DIRECTIONS: LISTEN. WRITE THE LETTERS IN THE BLANKS.

1. __ __ own
2. __ __ eater
3. __ __ ack
4. __ __ ant
5. __ __ een
6. __ __ ess
7. __ __ ow
8. __ __ ue

DIRECTIONS: LISTEN. CIRCLE THE LETTERS.

☺ sm   sn   sk   sw   (st)

1. cl   fl   bl   pl   gl
2. sh   th   wh   sn   ch
3. br   wh   dr   th   sw
4. gr   pl   br   gl   dr
5. pl   fr   gl   fl   gr
6. th   dr   wh   pl   sp
7. gr   br   dr   gl   fr
8. sk   sh   sp   ch   sw
9. sw   sm   sh   st   sn
10. gr   pl   bl   gl   cl

Blends and Digraphs IV
sl, tr, cr, fr, pr, kn, tw

zip

DIRECTIONS: READ AND WRITE.

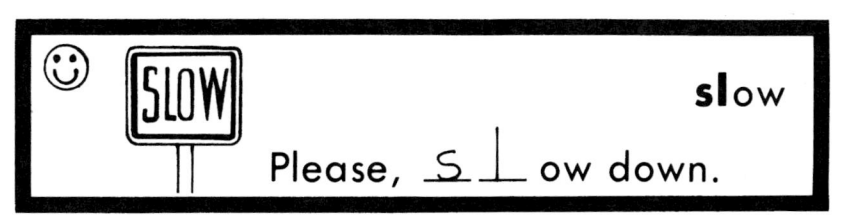

slow

Please, _sl_ ow down.

1. **tr**uck

No __ __ ucks.

2. **cr**edit

It's a __ __ edit card.

3. **fr**ies

I want __ __ ies.

4. **pr**esent

It's a __ __ esent.

5. **kn**ife

It's a __ __ ife.

6. **tw**enty

A: What's your age?
B: I'm __ __ enty.

69.

Blends and Digraphs IV

_____
home phone

DIRECTIONS: READ. CIRCLE THE LETTERS AND WRITE THEM IN THE BLANKS.

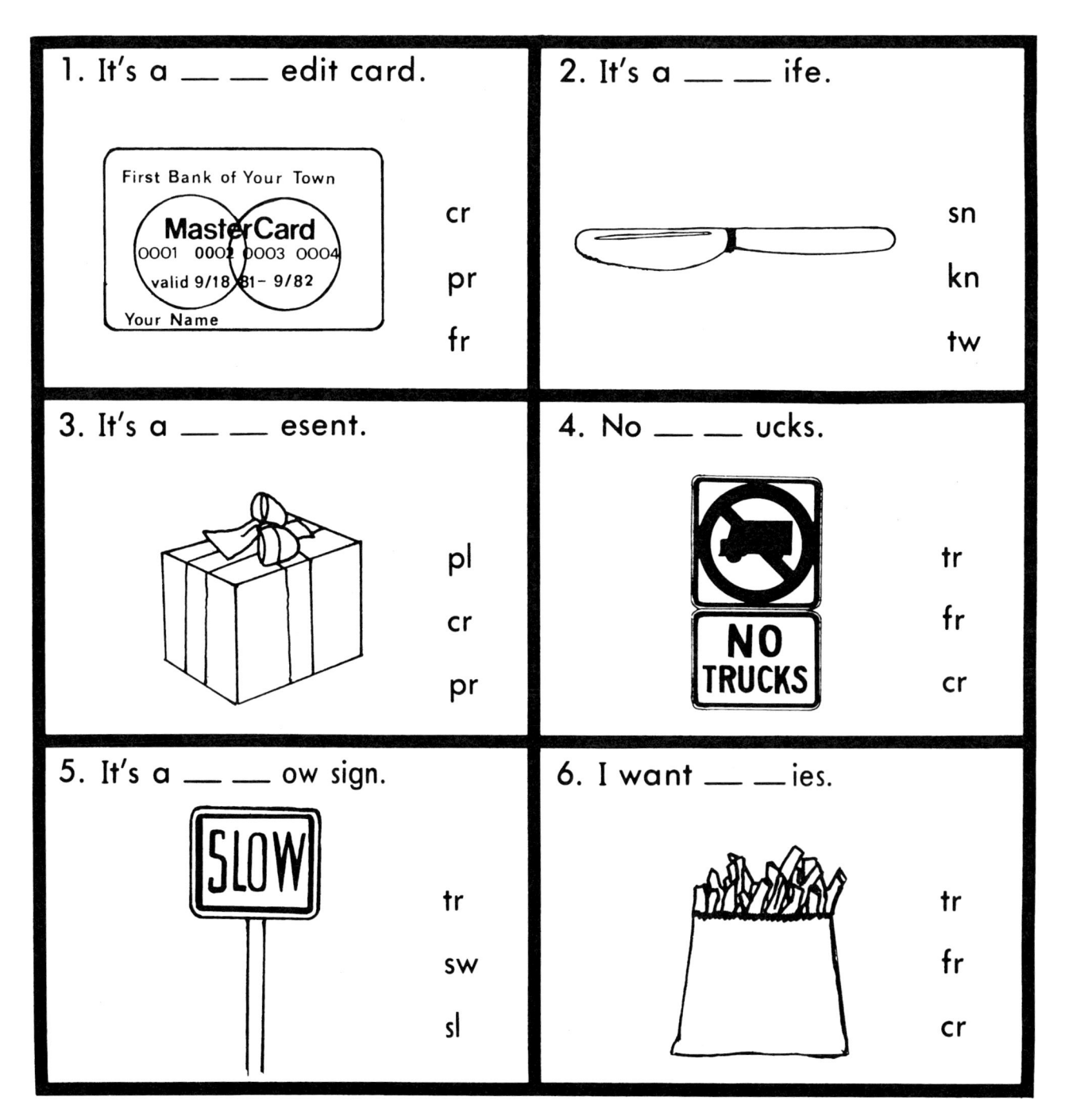

☺ I'm t̲ w̲ enty.   **20**   sw
sl
(tw)

1. It's a __ __ edit card.
   cr
   pr
   fr

2. It's a __ __ ife.
   sn
   kn
   tw

3. It's a __ __ esent.
   pl
   cr
   pr

4. No __ __ ucks.
   tr
   fr
   cr

5. It's a __ __ ow sign.
   tr
   sw
   sl

6. I want __ __ ies.
   tr
   fr
   cr

70.

Test
Blends and Digraphs I, II, III, IV

_____
last   first

DIRECTIONS: LISTEN. WRITE THE LETTERS IN THE BLANKS.

1. __ __ ife
2. __ __ ies
3. __ __ enty
4. __ __ uck

5. __ __ edit card
6. __ __ ow
7. __ __ esent
8. __ __ op

DIRECTIONS: WRITE THE LETTERS IN THE BLANKS.

1. 3 t h ree	2. __ __ one	3. __ __ ale
4. __ __ ant	5. __ __ ip	6. __ __ uck
7. __ __ ess	8. __ __ ife	9. __ __ een tree
10. __ __ air	11. __ __ ies	12. __ __ ag

71.

city   state

DIRECTIONS: WRITE THE LETTERS IN THE BLANKS.

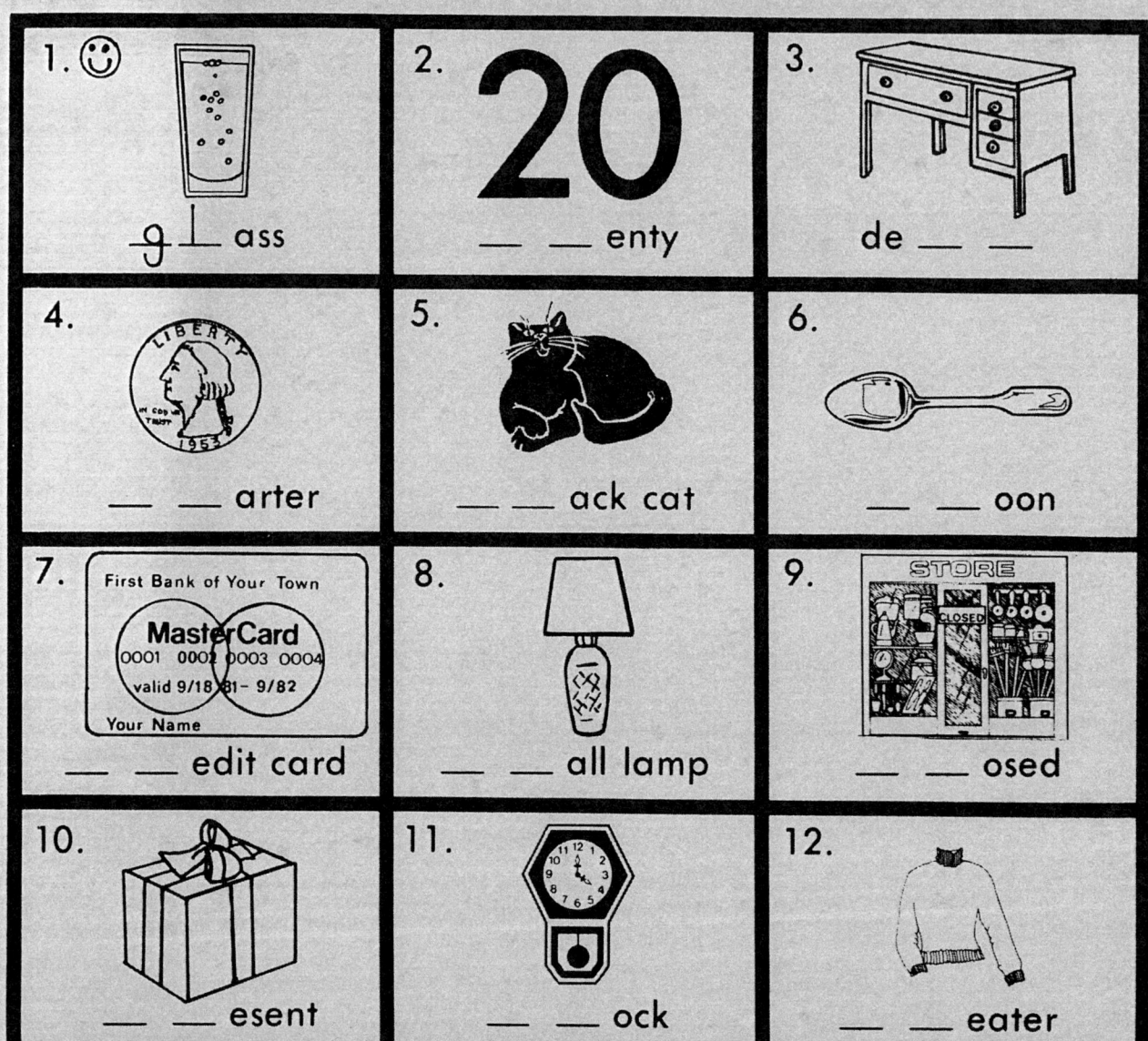

1. gl ass	2. __ __ enty	3. de __ __
4. __ __ arter	5. __ __ ack cat	6. __ __ oon
7. __ __ edit card	8. __ __ all lamp	9. __ __ osed
10. __ esent	11. __ __ ock	12. __ __ eater

DIRECTIONS: LISTEN AND WRITE.

1. _____

2. _____

3. _____

4. _____

72.

Letter Sequence

color of hair _____
color of eyes _____

The Alphabet

Aa	Bb	Cc	Dd	Ee	Ff	Gg
Hh	Ii	Jj	Kk	Ll	Mm	Nn
Oo	Pp	Qq	Rr	Ss	Tt	Uu
Vv	Ww	Xx	Yy	Zz		

DIRECTIONS: WRITE THE ALPHABET.

___ ___ ___ ___ ___ ___ Gg

___ ___ ___ ___ ___ Ll ___

___ Pp ___ ___ ___ ___ ___

Vv ___ ___ ___ ___ ___ ___

___ ___ ___ ___ ___ ___ ___

___ ___ ___ ___ ___ ___ ___

___ ___ ___ ___ ___ ___ ___

73.

Letter Sequence Capitals

Name _____

☐☐☐-☐☐-☐☐☐☐

DIRECTIONS: WRITE THE LETTER THAT COMES BEFORE OR AFTER.

A B   G H
___ N   A ___
___ Y   O ___
___ D   W ___
___ P   C ___
___ F   K ___
___ X   Q ___
G H   E ___
___ V   Y Z
___ J   U ___
___ Z   I ___
___ L   S ___
___ R   M ___

DIRECTIONS: WRITE THE ALPHABET.

___ ___ ___ ___ ___ ___ ___
___ ___ ___ ___ ___ ___ ___
___ ___ ___ ___ ___ ___ ___
___ ___ ___ ___ ___ ___ ___

Letter Sequence
Small letters

_____
address
_____

_____

DIRECTIONS: WRITE THE LETTERS IN ORDER.

a _b_ c   _d_ e _f_

p ___ r   ___ o ___

s ___ u   ___ x ___

t ___ v   ___ q ___

d ___ f   ___ s ___

j ___ l   ___ i ___

v ___ x   ___ d ___

h ___ j   ___ g ___

x ___ z   ___ t ___

g ___ i   ___ c ___

m ___ o   ___ k ___

l ___ n   ___ h ___

DIRECTIONS: WRITE THE ALPHABET.

___ ___ ___ ___ ___ ___

___ ___ ___ ___ ___ ___

___ ___ ___ ___ ___ ___

___ ___ ___ ___ ___

hair _____

eyes _____

Part 3 - Reading and Writing
Correlated to Lessons 1-10 of Delta's Effective ESL for the 21st Century Personal Information, continued

Lesson One, Section II
What is it?

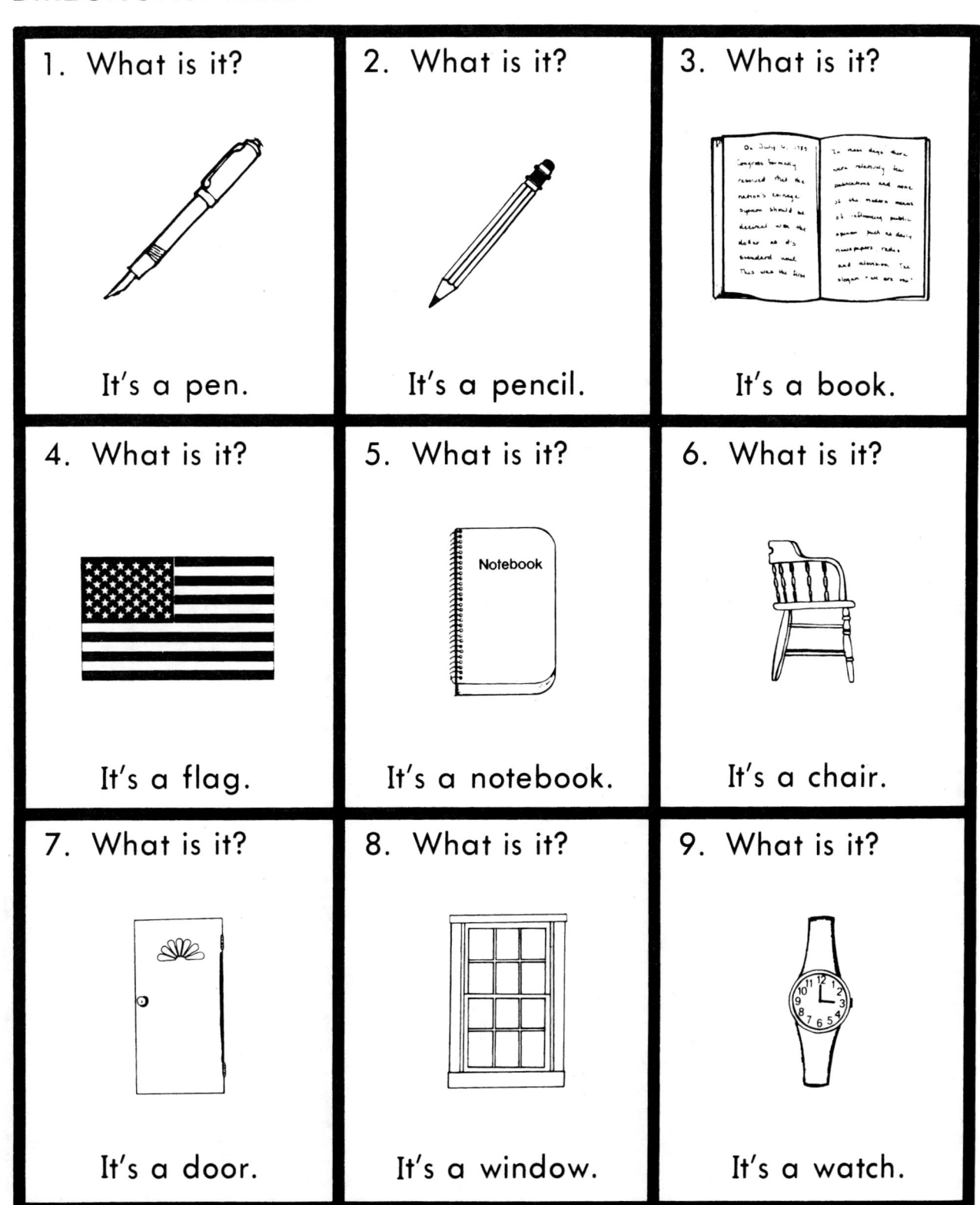

FIRST NAME _____

DIRECTIONS: READ.

1. What is it? It's a pen.	2. What is it? It's a pencil.	3. What is it? It's a book.
4. What is it? It's a flag.	5. What is it? It's a notebook.	6. What is it? It's a chair.
7. What is it? It's a door.	8. What is it? It's a window.	9. What is it? It's a watch.

color of eyes _____

DIRECTIONS: READ AND WRITE.

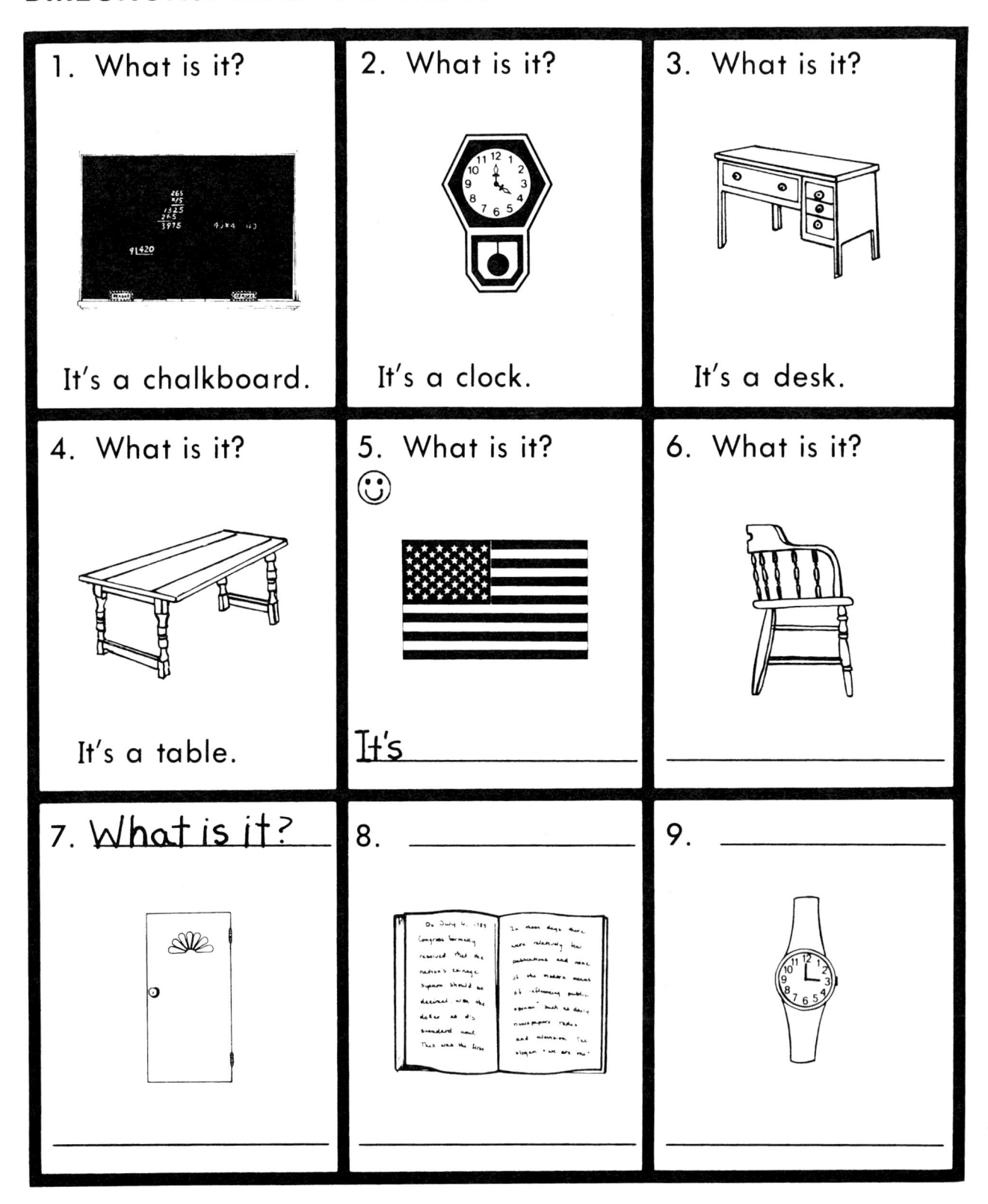

1. What is it?	2. What is it?	3. What is it?
It's a chalkboard.	It's a clock.	It's a desk.
4. What is it?	5. What is it? :)	6. What is it?
It's a table.	It's _____	
7. What is it?	8. _____	9. _____

80.

phone _____

DIRECTIONS: CIRCLE THE CORRECT ANSWER.

1. What is it?

   It's a pencil.
   (It's a pen.)
   It's a book.

2. What is it?

   It's a pen.
   It's a book.
   It's a pencil.

3. What is it?

   It's a pencil.
   It's a pen.
   It's a book.

4. What is it?

   It's a flag.
   It's a table.
   It's a desk.

5. What is it?

   It's a flag.
   It's a notebook.
   It's a chair.

6. What is it?

   It's a notebook.
   It's a flag.
   It's a chair.

7. What is it?

   It's a door.
   It's a window.
   It's a watch.

8. What is it?

   It's a door.
   It's a window.
   It's a watch.

9. What is it?

   It's a door.
   It's a window.
   It's a watch.

zip code _____

10. What is it?

It's a window.
It's a table.
It's a chalkboard.

11. What is it?

It's a clock.
It's a table.
It's a chair.

12. What is it?

It's a flag.
It's a table.
It's a desk.

13. What is it?

It's a flag.
It's a table.
It's a desk.

14. What is it?

It's a pencil.
It's a pen.
It's a pin.

15. What is it?

It's a flag.
It's a flug.
It's a fleg.

16. What is it?

It's a walch.
It's a wach.
It's a watch.

17. What is it?

It's a fable.
It's a table.
It's a tuble.

18. What is it?

It's a clack.
It's a cluck.
It's a clock.

Sex ☐ M
☐ F

DIRECTIONS: WRITE.

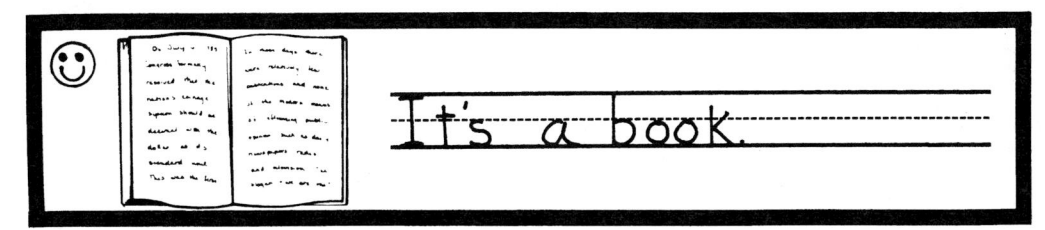

It's a book.

1.
2.
3.
4.
5.
6.

Mr.
Mrs. _____
Miss
Ms.

7.
8.
9.
10.
11.
12.
13.

84.

Lesson Two, Section I
What's your address?

Address
_____
_____

DIRECTIONS: READ.

1.
Mila: What's your address?
Bill: My address is 104 Fay Avenue.
Mila: What's your city?
Bill: My city's Los Angeles.
Mila: What's your zip code?
Bill: My zip code's 91107.

2.
Miss Mila Nelson
4710 Kenyon Street
Los Angeles, California 91104

Bill Brown
104 Fay Avenue
Los Angeles, California
91107

hair color

DIRECTIONS: READ.

1. What's Bill's address?

104 Fay Avenue

It's 104 Fay Avenue.

2. What's Bill's city?

Los Angeles,

It's Los Angeles.

3. What's Bill's state?

California

It's California.

4. What's Bill's zip code?

91107

It's 91107.

DIRECTIONS: READ AND WRITE.

My name's _____ . My address is _____ .
My city's _____ . My state's _____ . My zip code's _____ .

(___) ___-_____
area code   phone

DIRECTIONS: WRITE.

1. What's your name?

   My name's

2. What's your address?

   It's

3. What's your city?

   My city's

height

4. What's your state?

It's

5. What's your zip code?

It's

6. What's your phone number?

It's

7. My area code is

phone number ( ) ___-_____

DIRECTIONS: ADDRESS THE ENVELOPE TO ANOTHER STUDENT.

1.

DIRECTIONS: ADDRESS THE ENVELOPE TO YOUR TEACHER.

2.

Lesson Two, Section II
What time is it?

home phone
_____

DIRECTIONS: READ.

1.
A: Good morning, _____.
B: Good morning.
A: What time is it?
B: It's 6:00.
A: Thanks.

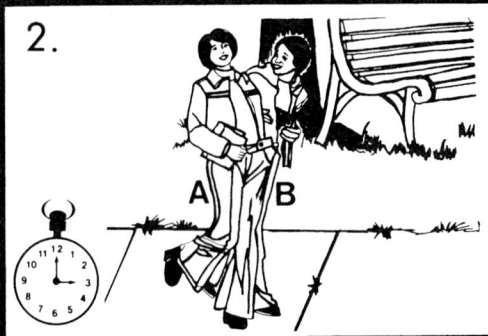

2.
A: Good afternoon, _____.
B: Hi, _____.
A: What time is it?
B: It's 3:00.
A: Thank you.

3.
A: Good evening, _____.
B: Hello, _____.
A: What time is it?
B: It's 8 o'clock.
A: Thank you.

4. Good afternoon. What time is it?

It's 1 o'clock.
It's 1:00.

5. Good afternoon. What time is it?

It's 2 o'clock.
It's 2:00.

6. Good afternoon. What time is it?

It's 3 o'clock.
It's 3:00.

area code _____

zip code _____

7. Good morning.
What time is it?

It's 9 o'clock.
It's 9:00.

8. Good morning.
What time is it?

It's 10 o'clock.
It's 10:00.

9. Good morning.
What time is it?

It's 11 o'clock.
It's 11:00.

10. Good afternoon.
What time is it?

It's 3 o'clock.
It's 3:00.

11. Good afternoon.
What time is it?

It's 4 o'clock.
It's 4:00.

12. Good afternoon.
What time is it?

It's 5 o'clock.
It's 5:00.

13. Good evening.
What time is it?

It's 6 o'clock.
It's 6:00.

14. Good evening.
What time is it?

It's 7 o'clock.
It's 7:00.

15. Good evening.
What time is it?

It's 8 o'clock.
It's 8:00.

height

DIRECTIONS: READ.

1.
A: Good morning, _____.
B: Good morning.
A: What time is it?
B: It's 6:30.
A: I'm early.

2.
A: Hello, _____.
B: Good afternoon.
A: What time is it?
B: It's 1:30.
A: I'm on time.

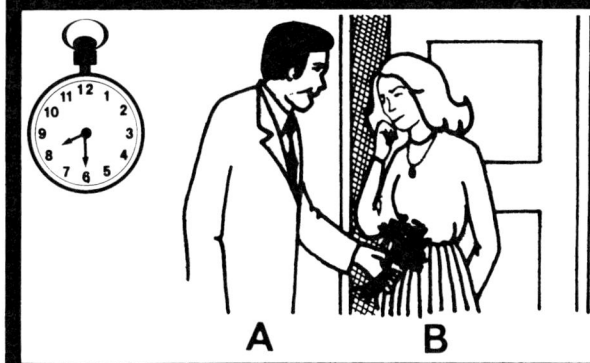

3.
A: Hi, _____.
B: Good evening.
A: What time is it?
B: It's 8:30.
A: I'm late. Sorry.

4. What time is it?
It's 1:30.
I'm early.

5. What time is it?
It's 2:30.
I'm on time.

6. What time is it?
It's 3:30.
I'm late.

It's _____ o'clock.

7. What time is it?	8. What time is it?	9. What time is it?
It's 4:30. I'm early.	It's 5:30. I'm on time.	It's 6:30. I'm late. Sorry.
10. What time is it?	11. What time is it?	12. What time is it?
It's 7:30. I'm early.	It's 8:30. I'm on time.	It's 9:30. I'm late. Sorry.
13. What time is it?	14. What time is it?	15. What time is it?
It's 10:30. I'm early.	It's 11:30. I'm on time.	It's 12:30. I'm late. Sorry.

☐ M   ☐ F

DIRECTIONS: CIRCLE THE CORRECT ANSWER.

1. What time is it?

   It's 3 o'clock.
   (It's 3:30.)
   It's 4:30.

2. What time is it?

   It's 6 o'clock.
   It's 6:30.
   It's 12:30.

3. What time is it?

   It's 9 o'clock.
   It's 9:30.
   It's 6:00.

4. What time is it?

   It's 5 o'clock.
   It's 5:30.
   It's 12:30.

5. What time is it?

   It's 9 o'clock.
   It's 3:00.
   It's 12:00.

6. What time is it?

   It's 10 o'clock.
   It's 12:00.
   It's 11:00.

7. What time is it?

   It's 4 o'clock.
   It's 4:30.
   It's 5:30.

8. What time is it?

   It's 6 o'clock.
   It's 5:30.
   It's 6:30.

9. What time is it?

   It's 7 o'clock.
   It's 12:30.
   It's 8:00.

area code   home phone

DIRECTIONS: CIRCLE THE CORRECT ANSWER.

1. What time is it?

   It's 2 o'clock.
   (It's 2:30.)
   It's 3:30.

2. What time is it?

   It's 12 o'clock.
   It's 12:30.
   It's 6:00.

3. What time is it?

   It's 12 o'clock.
   It's 12:30.
   It's 11:00.

4. What time is it?

   It's 12 o'clock.
   It's 12:30.
   It's 8:00.

5. What time is it?

   It's 2 o'clock.
   It's 2:30.
   It's 12:00.

6. What time is it?

   It's 6 o'clock.
   It's 7:30.
   It's 6:30.

7. What time is it?

   It's 6 o'clock.
   It's 12:30.
   It's 1:30.

8. What time is it?

   It's 6 o'clock.
   It's 8:30.
   It's 9:30.

9. What time is it?

   It's 11 o'clock.
   It's 10:00.
   It's 12:00.

height _____

DIRECTIONS: WRITE.

1. What time is it? 
 ☺
 It's 12:30.

2. _____

3. _____

4. _____

5. _____

6. _____

7. _____

8. _____

9. _____

hair	eyes

DIRECTIONS: DRAW THE HANDS.

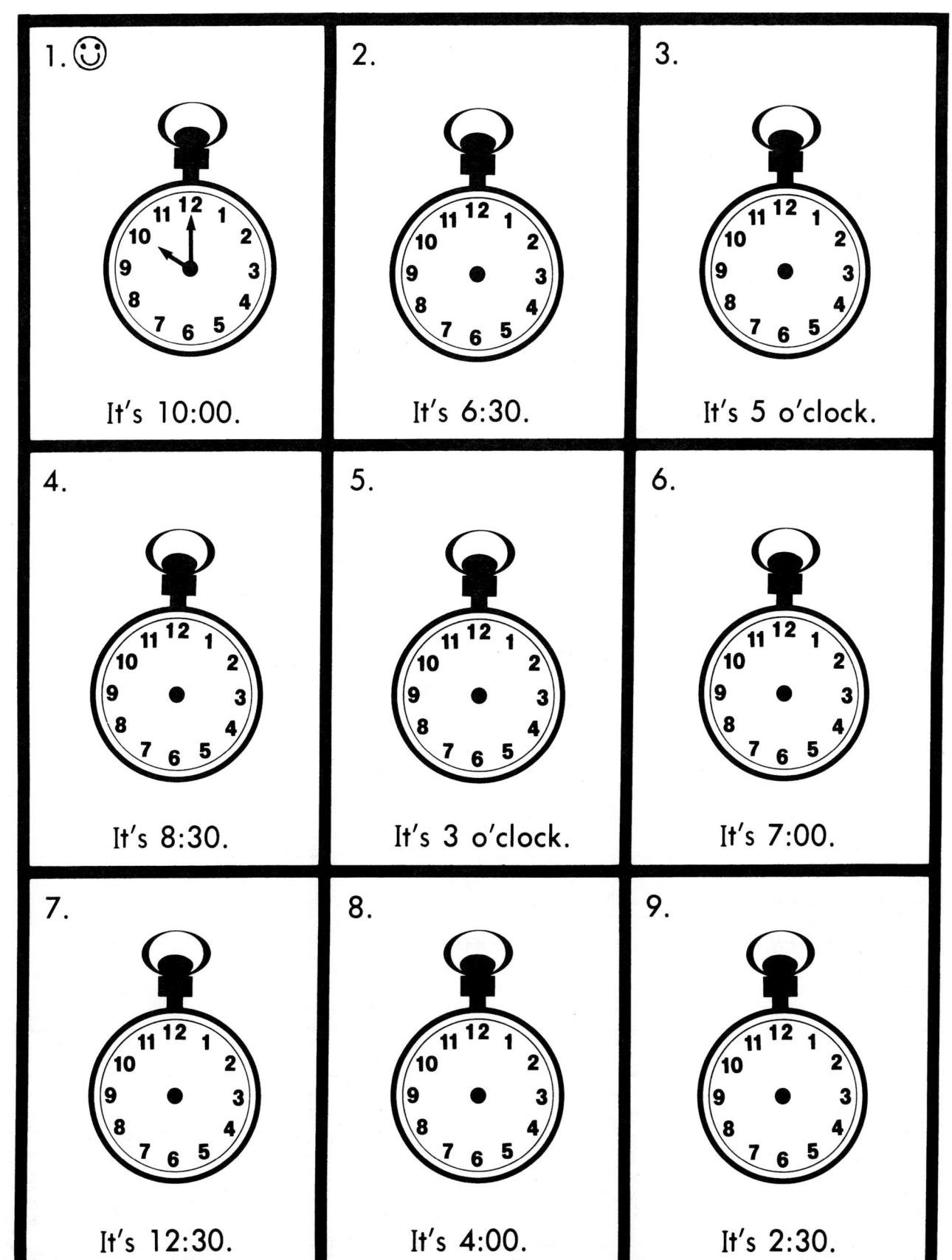

1. 🙂 It's 10:00.
2. It's 6:30.
3. It's 5 o'clock.
4. It's 8:30.
5. It's 3 o'clock.
6. It's 7:00.
7. It's 12:30.
8. It's 4:00.
9. It's 2:30.

Mr.
Mrs.
Miss
Ms.

Lesson Three, Section I
What is he/she?

_____
city   state   zip

DIRECTIONS: READ.

1. 
   A: What is he?
   B: He's a doctor.
   A: What is she?
   B: She's a nurse.

2. What is he? 
   He's a busboy.

3. What is she? 
   She's a nurse.

4. What is he? 
   He's a waiter.

5. What is he? 
   He's a cook.

6. What is she? 
   She's a housewife.

7. What is he? 
   He's a gardener.

8. What is she? 
   She's a secretary.

9. What is he? 
   He's a salesman.

10. What is she? 
    She's a saleslady.

Age _____

DIRECTIONS: READ.

1. Is he a gardener?

Yes, he is.

Is he a gardener?

No, he isn't.

2. Is he a doctor?

Yes, he is.

Is he a doctor?

No, he isn't.

3. Is she a housewife?

Yes, she is.

Is she a housewife?

No, she isn't.

4. Is he a cook?

Yes, he is.

Is he a cook?

No, he isn't.

5. Is she a nurse?

Yes, she is.

Is she a nurse?

No, she isn't.

6. Is he a waiter?

Yes, he is.

Is he a waiter?

No, he isn't.

weight

DIRECTIONS: YES OR NO? WRITE.

1. Is she a nurse?
   No, she isn't.

2. Is he a waiter?
   _____

3. Is she a nurse?
   _____

4. Is he a gardener?
   _____

5. Is she a saleslady?
   _____

6. Is he a busboy?
   _____

7. Is she a housewife?
   _____

( ) -

DIRECTIONS: READ.

1.
A: Is she a housewife?
B: No, she isn't.
A: What is she?
B: She's a nurse.

2. Is she a doctor?
No, she isn't. 
What is she?
She's a saleslady.

3. Is she a nurse?
No, she isn't. 
What is she?
She's a secretary.

4. Is he a cook?
No, he isn't. 
What is he?
He's a salesman.

5. ☺ 
Is he a salesman?
No, _____.
What is he?
_____.

6. 
Is she a saleslady?
___ , _____.
_____?
_____.

soc. sec. number

DIRECTIONS: CIRCLE THE CORRECT ANSWER.

1. What is he?

   He's a gardener.
   He's a waiter.
   (He's a doctor.)

2. What is she?

   She's a nurse.
   She's a secretary.
   She's a saleslady.

3. What is he?

   He's a cook.
   He's a waiter.
   He's a salesman.

4. What is she?

   She's a housewife.
   She's a saleslady.
   She's a secretary.

5. What is he?

   He's a salesman.
   He's a doctor.
   He's a waiter.

6. What is she?

   She's a saleslady.
   She's a housewife.
   She's a secretary.

7. What is he?

   He's a gardener.
   He's a salesman.
   He's a waiter.

8. What is she?

   She's a nurse.
   She's a housewife.
   She's a secretary.

9. What is he?

   He's a salesman.
   He's a waiter.
   He's a gardener.

Address _____
_____
_____

DIRECTIONS: WRITE.

1. ☺ What is he?
   He's a doctor.
   doctor

2. ☺ What is she?
   She's a nurse.
   nurse

3. What is she?
   _____
   secretary

4. What is he?
   _____
   waiter

height_____weight_____

5. salesman — What is he? _____

6. saleslady — What is she? _____

7. housewife — What is she? _____

8. cook — What is he? _____

9. gardener — What is he? _____

105.

Mr. ☐   Miss ☐
Mrs. ☐ Ms. ☐

DIRECTIONS: CIRCLE THE CORRECT ANSWER.

1. Is she a nurse? 
(No, she isn't.)
Yes, she is.
Yes, he is.

2. Is he a doctor? 
Yes, he is.
No, he isn't.
Yes, she is.

3. Is she a secretary? 
Yes, she is.
No, she isn't.
No, he isn't.

4. Is he a salesman? 
No, he isn't.
Yes, she is.
Yes, he is.

5. Is she a nurse? 
Yes, she is.
No, she isn't.
No, he isn't.

6. Is he a gardener? 
Yes, she is.
Yes, he is.
No, he isn't.

7. Is she a secretary? 
Yes, he is.
No, she isn't.
Yes, she is.

8. Is he a waiter? 
Yes, she is.
No, he isn't.
Yes, he is.

9. Is she a housewife? 
Yes, he is.
Yes, she is.
No, she isn't.

106.

Lesson Three, Section II
What's his/her name?

Sex ☐ M ☐ F

DIRECTIONS: READ.

1.
A: What's his name?
B: His name's Ben.
A: What's her name?
B: Her name's Ann.

DIRECTIONS: READ AND WRITE.

2.
Her name's Ann.
She's a secretary.
Her address is 512 Union Ave.

1. What's her name? __Her__ _____
2. What is she? __She's__ _____
3. What's her address? __It's__ _____

3.
His name's Tom.
He's a gardener.
His address is 3765 First Street.

1. What's his name? _____
2. What is he? _____
3. What's his address? _____

Odd Man Out

☐ 15-19 ☐ 30-39 ☐ 50-59
☐ 20-29 ☐ 40-49 ☐ 60-69
         ☐ 70-79

DIRECTIONS: LISTEN AND PUT AN X ON THE ONE THAT IS DIFFERENT.

| ☺ | city | ~~time~~ | state | zip code | address |

1. name	address	phone	pencil	age
2. pen	desk	man	lamp	table
3. Sam	bed	Ben	Jan	Kay
4. 6:00	3:30	1:30	12:30	6:30
5. doctor	nurse	waiter	cook	flag
6. Good evening.	I'm early.	Good morning.	Hello.	Good afternoon.
7. home phone	social security	age	sick	area code
8. gardener	window	watch	book	door
9. Mr.	Mrs.	mall	Miss	Ms.
10. gl	pr	th	wh	ss

108.

Lesson Four, Section I
What are they?

☐☐☐ – ☐☐ – ☐☐☐☐

DIRECTIONS: READ.

1. What are they? 
They're teachers.

2. What are they? 
They're barbers.

3. What are they? 
They're lawyers.

DIRECTIONS: WRITE.

4. students
What are they?
They're students.

5. bakers
What are they?
_____

6. dentists
What are they?
_____

109.

zip code

DIRECTIONS: WRITE.

1. a baker / bakers

What is he?
He's a baker.

What are they?
They're bakers.

2. a teacher / teachers

What is she?
_____

What are they?
_____

3. a student / students

What is he?
_____

What are they?
_____

It's _____

4.
a lawyer

What is he?
_____

lawyers

What are they?
_____

5.
a barber

What _____?
_____

barbers

What _____?
_____

6.
a dentist

_____
_____

dentists

_____
_____

111.

DIRECTIONS: READ.

1. Are they lawyers?

   Yes, they are.

2. Are they students?

   Yes, they are.

3. Are they teachers?

   Yes, they are.

4. Are they busboys?

   No, they aren't.

5. Are they students?

   No, they aren't.

6. Are they cooks?

   No, they aren't.

7. Are they dentists?

   Yes, they are.

8. Are they barbers?

   Yes, they are.

9. Are they nurses?

   No, they aren't.

It's _____

DIRECTIONS: CIRCLE THE CORRECT ANSWER.

1. Are they students? 
   Yes, they are.
   (No, they aren't.)
   No, he isn't.

2. Is he a busboy? 
   No, he isn't.
   No, they aren't.
   No, she isn't.

3. Is she a teacher? 
   Yes, they are.
   Yes, she is.
   Yes, he is.

4. Is he a waiter? 
   No, he isn't.
   Yes, he is.
   Yes, they are.

5. Are they barbers? 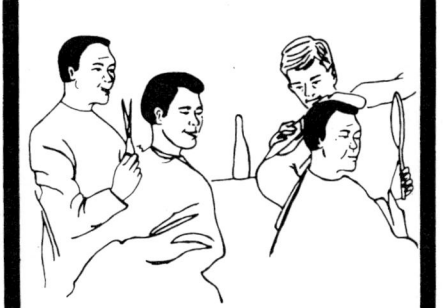
   Yes, they are.
   No, they aren't.
   No, she isn't.

6. Are they lawyers? 
   No, they aren't.
   No, she isn't.
   No, he isn't.

7. Is he a dentist? 
   Yes, he is.
   No, he isn't.
   Yes, she is.

8. Are they busboys? 
   Yes, they are.
   No, they aren't.
   Yes, he is.

9. Are they waiters? 
   No, they aren't.
   No, she isn't.
   Yes, they are.

It's ____:____ .

DIRECTIONS: READ.

1. Lucy and Al are students. They aren't teachers. Dick isn't a student. He's a teacher.

DIRECTIONS: READ AND WRITE.

2. Are Lucy and Al teachers?
No,_____

Are they students?
_____

3. Is Dick a student?
_____

Is he a teacher?
_____

114.

Age _____

___ M ___ F

DIRECTIONS: READ.

1. 
A: Are they teachers?
B: No, they aren't.
A: What are they?
B: They're students.

2. Are they dentists?
No, they aren't. 
What are they?
They're lawyers.

3. Are they teachers?
No, they aren't. 
What are they?
They're bakers.

4. Are they students?
No, they aren't. 
What are they?
They're waiters.

DIRECTIONS: READ AND WRITE.

5. Are they teachers?
No, _____ 
What are they?
They're _____

6. Are they cooks? 
_____
What are they?
_____

7. Are they lawyers? 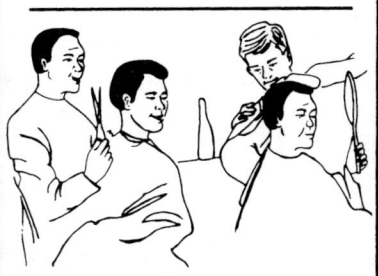
_____
What are they?
_____

115.

Lesson Four, Section II　　　　　　　　　　　　　hair color _____
Where are you from?

DIRECTIONS: READ AND WRITE.

1. 
   A: Where are you from?
   B: I'm from Japan.
   A: Are you Japanese?
   B: Yes, I am. I'm Japanese.

2. My name's Joe Gomez. My first name's Joe. My last name's Gomez. I'm from Mexico. My country's Mexico. I'm Mexican.

3. 
   A: What country are you from?
   B: We're from China.
   A: What are you?
   B: We're Chinese.

4. 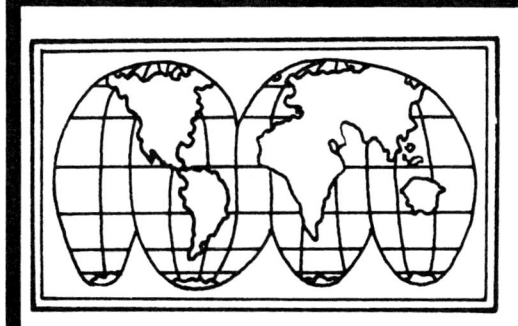
   Where are you from?
   I'm from _____
   What are you?
   I'm _____

116.

birthplace

DIRECTIONS: CIRCLE THE CORRECT ANSWER.

1. Where is he from?

She's from Mexico.
He's from Mexico.
They're from Mexico.

2. Where is she from?

She's from Japan.
He's from Japan.
They're from Japan.

3. Where are you from?

She's from China.
I'm from China.
We're from China.

DIRECTIONS: WRITE.

4. Where are you from?

I'm from _____ .
I'm _____ .

5. What country are you from?

I'm from _____ .
I'm _____ .

6. What's your birthplace?

It's _____ .
I'm _____ .

7. What are you?

I'm _____

Contractions   Country _____

DIRECTIONS: WRITE THE SHORT FORM.

1. I am   ☺ I'm

2. you are

3. are not

4. he is

5. she is

6. it is

7. is not

8. we are

9. they are

10. what is

11. name is

birthplace

DIRECTIONS: WRITE THE LONG FORM.

1. I'm ☺ I am
2. you're
3. aren't
4. he's
5. she's
6. it's
7. isn't
8. we're
9. they're
10. what's
11. name's

height _____ weight _____

Lesson Five, Section I
What time is it?

Address _____
_____

DIRECTIONS: READ.

1. 
A: Good evening, _____ .
B: Hello, _____ .
A: What time is it?
B: It's 7:15.
A: I'm on time.

2. What time is it? 
It's 1:15.
I'm early.

3. What time is it? 
It's 2:15.
I'm on time.

4. What time is it? 
It's 3:15.
I'm late.

5. What time is it? 
It's 4:15.
I'm early.

6. What time is it? 
It's 5:15.
I'm on time.

7. What time is it? 
It's 6:15.
I'm late.

_____

country

DIRECTIONS: READ.

1.
A: Excuse me.
   Is it 6:15?
B: Yes, it is.
A: Thanks.

2. Is it 7:15?
Yes, it is.
Thanks.

3. Is it 8:15?
Yes, it is.
Thank you.

4. Is it 9:15?
Yes, it is.
Thanks.

5. Is it 10:15?
Yes, it is.
Thank you.

6. Is it 11:15?
Yes, it is.
Thanks.

7. Is it 12:15?
Yes, it is.
Thank you.

last   first   middle

DIRECTIONS: READ.

1. A: What time is it?
B: It's 12:45.
A: Good night, _____ .
B: Good night, _____ .
How time flies.

2. What time is it?
It's 1:45.
How time flies.

3. What time is it?
It's 2:45.
Thanks.

4. What time is it?
It's 3:45.
How time flies.

5. What time is it?
It's 4:45.
Thank you.

6. What time is it?
It's 8:45.
How time flies.

7. What time is it?
It's 10:45.
I'm late.

middle name

DIRECTIONS: CIRCLE THE CORRECT ANSWER.

1. What time is it?	2. What time is it?	3. What time is it?
It's 2:15. (It's 3:15.)	It's 5:45. It's 9:30.	It's 3:00. It's 12:15.
4. What time is it?	5. What time is it?	6. What time is it?
It's 1:45. It's 9:15.	It's 3:00. It's 11:15.	It's 3:45. It's 4:45.
7. What time is it?	8. What time is it?	9. What time is it?
It's 3:30. It's 6:15.	It's 8:45. It's 7:45.	It's 3:45. It's 10:15.

( ) —
Area code   telephone

DIRECTIONS: WRITE.

☺ 1. What time is it?

It's 4:45.

2. What time is it?

_____

3. What time is it?

_____

4. What time is it?

_____

5. What time is it?

_____

6. What time is it?

_____

☺ 7. What_____

_____

8. _____

_____

125.

I'm from _____

DIRECTIONS: DRAW THE HANDS.

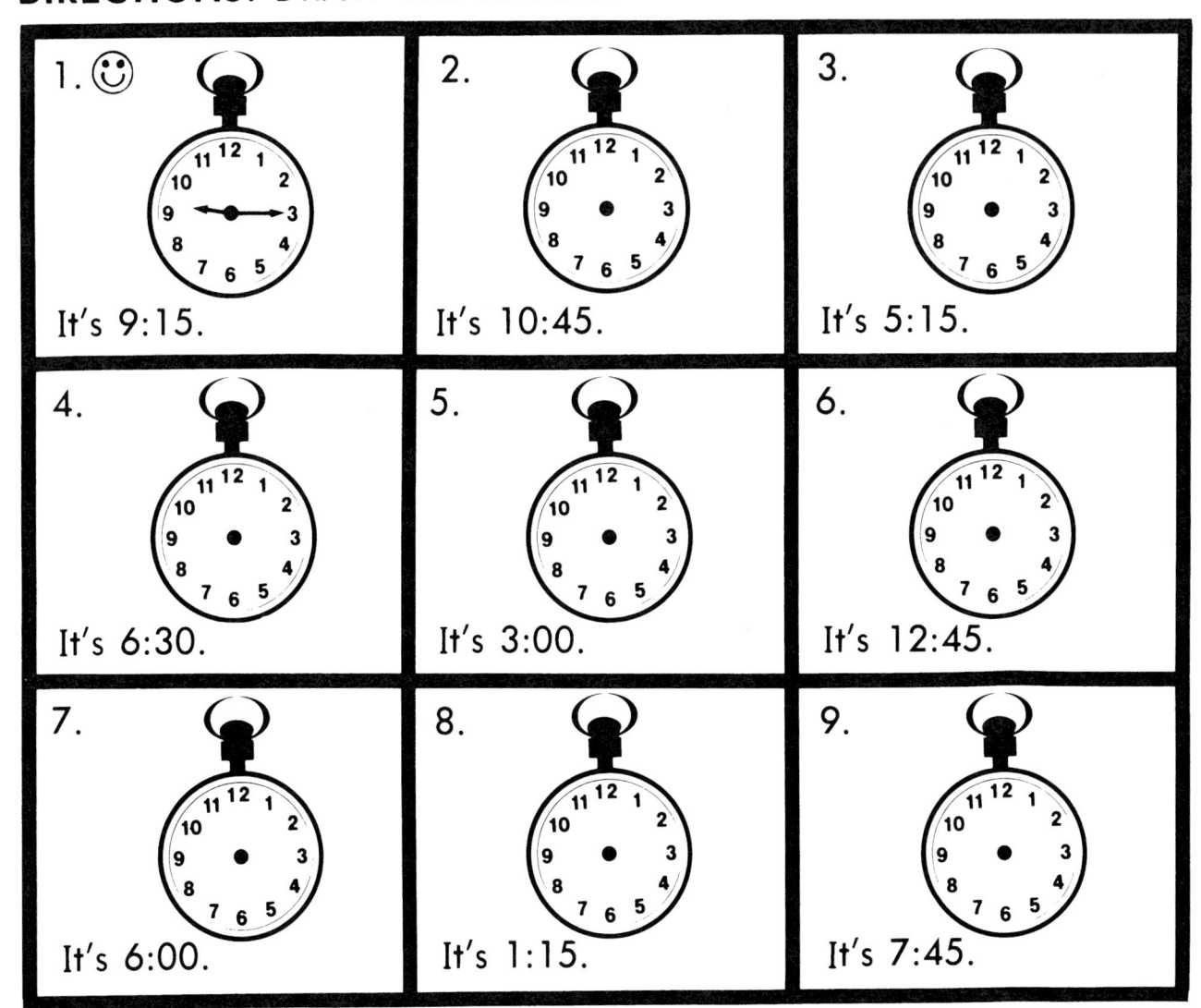

1. ☺ It's 9:15.	2. It's 10:45.	3. It's 5:15.
4. It's 6:30.	5. It's 3:00.	6. It's 12:45.
7. It's 6:00.	8. It's 1:15.	9. It's 7:45.

DIRECTIONS: LISTEN AND WRITE.

1. _____
2. _____
3. _____
4. _____
5. _____

Extension
  Where are you from?

Time _____

DIRECTIONS: READ.

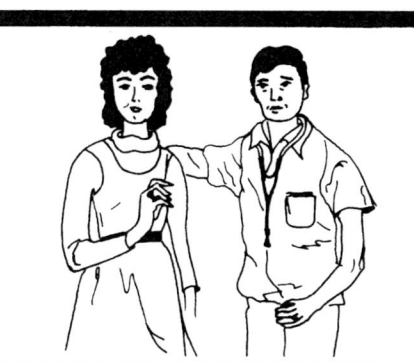

1. Mr. and Mrs. Lee are married. Mr. Lee is from Korea. He's Korean. He's a doctor. Mrs. Lee is from France. She's French. She's a housewife.

2. Joe and Lucy are single. They're from Mexico. They're Mexican. They're students.

3. My name is Suzuko. I'm married. I'm from Japan. I'm a secretary.

DIRECTIONS: WRITE ABOUT YOURSELF OR SOMEONE ELSE.

_____
_____
_____
_____
_____

Lesson Five, Section II
What day is it?

☐ married
☐ single

DIRECTIONS: READ.

1.
A: Hi. How are you?
B: Fine, thank you.
A: What day is it?
B: It's Tuesday.

2.

MARCH						
Sun.	Mon.	Tues.	Wed.	Thur.	Fri.	Sat.
1	2	3	4	5	6	7
8	9	10	11	12	13	14
15	16	17	18	19	20	21
22	23	24	25	26	27	28
29	30	31				

Sunday-Sun.
Monday-Mon.
Tuesday-Tues.
Wednesday-Wed.
Thursday-Thur.
Friday-Fri.
Saturday-Sat.

3.
A: Is today Wednesday?
B: No, it isn't.
A: What day is it?
B: It is Thursday.

☐ married ☐ divorced
☐ single   ☐ widowed

DIRECTIONS: READ.

1. What day is it?

MARCH						
Sun.	Mon.	Tues.	Wed.	Thur.	Fri.	Sat.
X						

   It's Sunday.

2. What day is it?

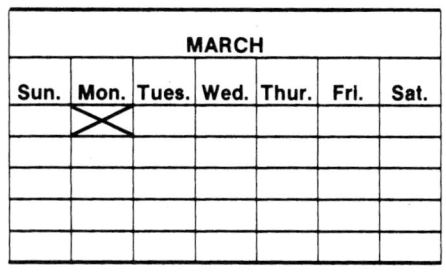

MARCH						
Sun.	Mon.	Tues.	Wed.	Thur.	Fri.	Sat.
	X					

   It's Monday.

3. What day is it?

MARCH						
Sun.	Mon.	Tues.	Wed.	Thur.	Fri.	Sat.
		X				

   It's Tuesday.

4. What day is it?

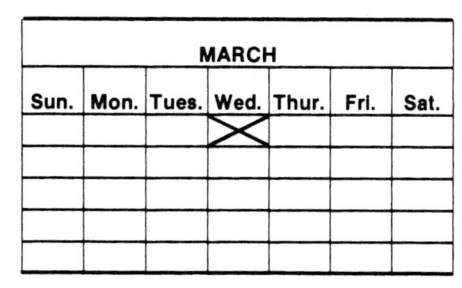

MARCH						
Sun.	Mon.	Tues.	Wed.	Thur.	Fri.	Sat.
			X			

   It's Wednesday.

5. What day is it?

MARCH						
Sun.	Mon.	Tues.	Wed.	Thur.	Fri.	Sat.
				X		

   It's Thursday.

6. What day is it?

MARCH						
Sun.	Mon.	Tues.	Wed.	Thur.	Fri.	Sat.
					X	

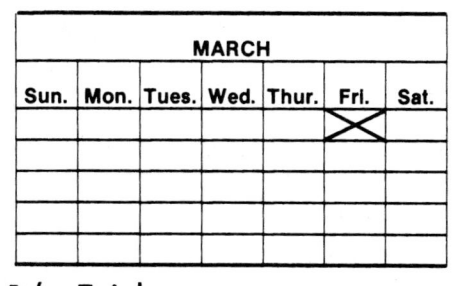

   It's Friday.

7. What day is it?

MARCH						
Sun.	Mon.	Tues.	Wed.	Thur.	Fri.	Sat.
						X

   It's Saturday.

8. What day is today?

Sun.	Mon.	Tues.	Wed.	Thur.	Fri.	Sat.

   It's _____

date of birth ___ - ___ - ___

DIRECTIONS: CIRCLE THE CORRECT ANSWER.

1. What day is it?

MARCH						
Sun.	Mon.	Tues.	Wed.	Thur.	Fri.	Sat.
				X		

   It's Tuesday.
   (It's Thursday.)
   It's Friday.

2. What day is it?

MARCH						
Sun.	Mon.	Tues.	Wed.	Thur.	Fri.	Sat.
					X	

   It's Friday.
   It's Tuesday.
   It's Thursday.

3. What day is it?

MARCH						
Sun.	Mon.	Tues.	Wed.	Thur.	Fri.	Sat.
X						

   It's Saturday.
   It's Monday.
   It's Sunday.

4. What day is it?

MARCH						
Sun.	Mon.	Tues.	Wed.	Thur.	Fri.	Sat.
						X

   It's Saturday.
   It's Sunday.
   It's Friday.

5. What day is it?

MARCH						
Sun.	Mon.	Tues.	Wed.	Thur.	Fri.	Sat.
		X				

   It's Thursday.
   It's Tuesday.
   It's Friday.

6. What day is it?

MARCH						
Sun.	Mon.	Tues.	Wed.	Thur.	Fri.	Sat.
			X			

   It's Monday.
   It's Wednesday.
   It's Thursday.

7. What day is it?

MARCH						
Sun.	Mon.	Tues.	Wed.	Thur.	Fri.	Sat.
	X					

   It's Friday.
   It's Wednesday.
   It's Monday.

8. What day is it today?

MARCH						
Sun.	Mon.	Tues.	Wed.	Thur.	Fri.	Sat.

   It's _____

birthdate ___/___/___

DIRECTIONS: WRITE.

☺ 1. What day is it?

MARCH						
Sun.	Mon.	Tues.	Wed.	Thur.	Fri.	Sat.
✗						

It's Sunday.

2. What day is it?

MARCH						
Sun.	Mon.	Tues.	Wed.	Thur.	Fri.	Sat.
	✗					

_____

3. What day is it?

MARCH						
Sun.	Mon.	Tues.	Wed.	Thur.	Fri.	Sat.
		✗				

_____

4. What day is it?

MARCH						
Sun.	Mon.	Tues.	Wed.	Thur.	Fri.	Sat.
			✗			

_____

5. What day is it?

MARCH						
Sun.	Mon.	Tues.	Wed.	Thur.	Fri.	Sat.
				✗		

_____

6. What day is it?

MARCH						
Sun.	Mon.	Tues.	Wed.	Thur.	Fri.	Sat.
					✗	

_____

7. What day is it?

MARCH						
Sun.	Mon.	Tues.	Wed.	Thur.	Fri.	Sat.
						✗

_____

8. What day is it today?

Sun.	Mon.	Tues.	Wed.	Thur.	Fri.	Sat.

_____

Sentence scramble   Today is _____

DIRECTIONS: UNSCRAMBLE

☺ on   I'm   time.

I'm on time.

1. a   Is   he   salesman?
   _____

2. day   today?   is   What   it
   _____

3. are   Mr.   Lee   and   Mrs.   married.
   _____

4. time   it?   What   is
   _____

5. from   They're   Mexico.
   _____

6. are   from?   Where   you
   _____

7. Avenue.   Her   512   address   Union   is
   _____

8. phone   What's   number?   your
   _____

9. a   salesman.   isn't   He
   _____

10. 7:45?   Is   it
    _____

132.

Test, Lessons 1-5

_____ _____
                last   first

DIRECTIONS: READ AND WRITE.

1. What is it? _____

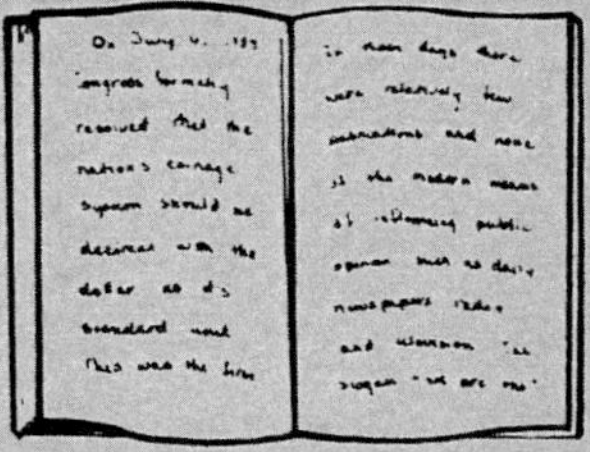

2. What is it? _____

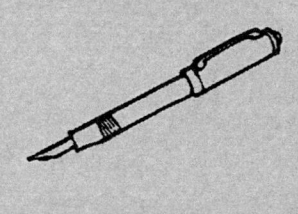

3. What time is it? _____

4. What time is it? _____

5. What time is it? _____

6. What time is it? _____

7. Where are you from? _____

8. What day is it today? _____

DIRECTIONS: DRAW THE HANDS.

9. It's 5:30.

10. It's 9:00.

11. It's 11:45.

133.

age	height	weight

DIRECTIONS: CIRCLE THE CORRECT ANSWER.

1. 
Good morning.
Good afternoon.
Good evening.

2. 
Good morning.
Good afternoon.
Good evening.

3. 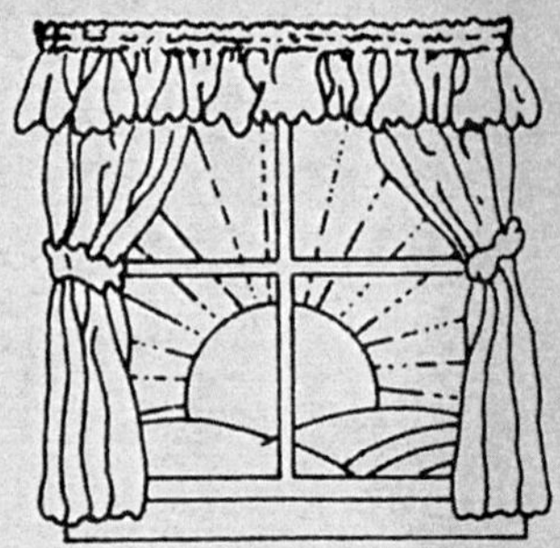
Good morning.
Good afternoon.
Good evening.

4. 
I'm early.
I'm on time.
I'm late.

5. 
I'm early.
I'm on time.
I'm late.

6. 
I'm early.
I'm on time.
I'm late.

7. What is she? 
She's a housewife.
She's a nurse.
She's a secretary.

8. What is he? 
He's a waiter.
He's a busboy.
He's a cook.

9. What is he? 
He's a saleslady.
He's a salesman.
He's a gardener.

| hair | eyes |

DIRECTIONS: CIRCLE THE CORRECT ANSWER.

1. Is she a nurse?

   Yes, she's.
   Yes, she is.
   Yes, he is.

2. What is she?
   What is it?
   What is he?

   He's a doctor.

3. Is he a waiter?

   No, he isn't.
   No, he is.
   Yes, he isn't.

4. What are they?

   They're barbers.
   They're dentists.
   He is doctors.

5. Are they lawyers?

   Yes, they are.
   Yes, they're.
   Yes, they aren't.

6. Are they teachers?

   No, they are.
   No, they're.
   No, they aren't.

7. Is they dentists?
   Are dentists?
   Are they dentists?

   Yes, they are.

8. It's Saturday.

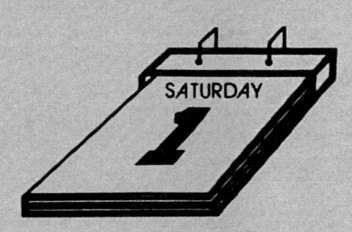

   Satur.
   Sat.
   Satu.

9. It's Thursday.

   Thurs.
   Thur.
   Thu.

135.

_____ birthplace

DIRECTIONS: LISTEN AND WRITE.

1. _____
2. _____
3. _____
4. _____
5. _____

DIRECTIONS: CHANGE TO THE SHORT FORM.

☺

1. It is   It's _____   5. they are _____
2. are not _____   6. she is   _____
3. is not   _____   7. I am   _____
4. we are   _____   8. you are _____

Mr.
Mrs.   **APPLICATION**
Miss   _____
Ms.   last   first   middle
        _____
        address
__ M   _____
__ F   city   state   zip code

date of birth	age	country	Office Use Only
area code	home phone	(circle) married single divorced widowed	9 9 9 9 9 9 9 9 9 7 6 5 4 3 2 1 0 8
soc. sec. no. ___-__-____	height	weight	hair color	eye color

136.

Lesson Six, Section I
How much is it?

Today is _____

DIRECTIONS: READ.

1. What's this? It's a penny. How much is it? It's 1 cent.	2. What's this? It's a nickel. How much is it? It's 5 cents.	3. What's this? It's a dime. How much is it? It's 10 cents.
4. What's this? It's a quarter. How much is it? It's 25 cents.	5. What's this? It's a half dollar. How much is it? It's 50 cents.	6. What's this? It's a dollar. How much is it? It's 100 cents.

How much is it?

a penny	=	1 cent	=	1¢	= $ .01
a nickel	=	5 cents	=	5¢	= $ .05
a dime	=	10 cents	=	10¢	= $ .10
a quarter	=	25 cents	=	25¢	= $ .25
a half dollar	=	50 cents	=	50¢	= $ .50
a dollar	=	100 cents	=	100¢	= $1.00

signature _____

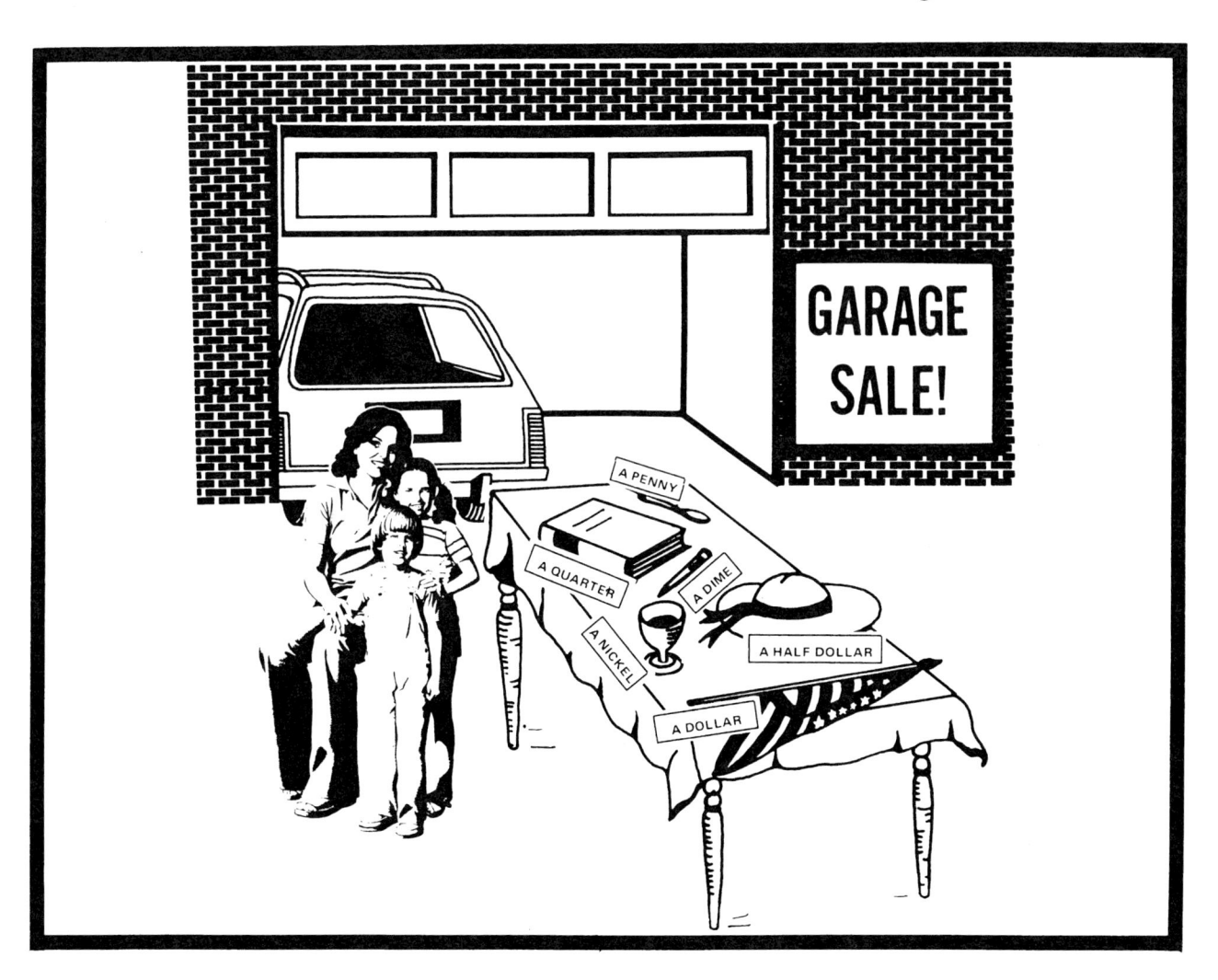

DIRECTIONS: WRITE.

1. How much is the pen?

2. How much is the book?

3. How much is the hat?

4. How much is the glass?

5. How much is the flag?

6. How much is the spoon?

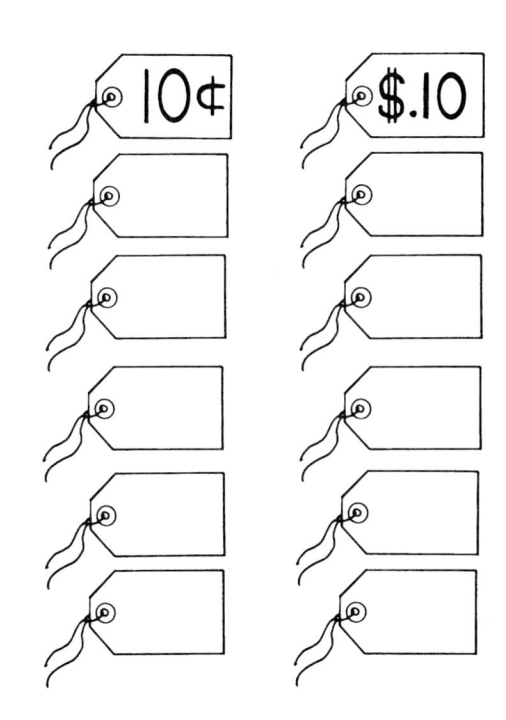

Social Security Number

DIRECTIONS: READ.

A: Excuse me, what's this?
B: It's a hamburger.
A: How much is it?
B: It's $1.10.

DIRECTIONS: READ AND WRITE.

1. What's this?
   It's a hot dog.

   How much is it?

   It's _____.

2. What's this?
   It's a soft drink.

   How much is it?

   It's _____.

3. What's this?
   It's a doughnut.

   How much is it?

   It's _____.

country

4. What's this?
It's a hamburger.

How much is it?

It's _____ .

5. What's this?
It's a cup of tea.

How much is it?

It's _____ .

6. What's this?
It's a pencil.

How much is it?

It's _____ .

7. What's this?
It's a pen.

How much is it?

It's _____ .

8. What's this?
It's a cup of coffee.

How much is it?

It's _____ .

9. What's this?
It's a book.

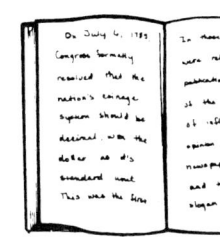

How much is it?

It's _____ .

140.

Review   Today is _____

DIRECTIONS: LISTEN AND WRITE.

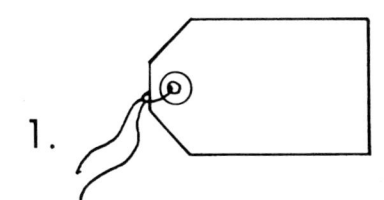

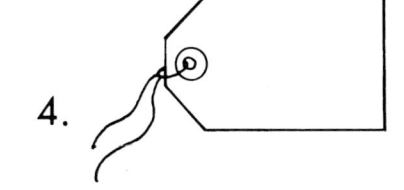

1.   2.   3.

4.   5.   6.

DIRECTIONS: CIRCLE THE CORRECT ANSWER.

1. A penny is (1 cent) 5 cents 10 cents	2. A dime is 1 cent 5 cents 10 cents	3. A quarter is 25 cents 10 cents 5 cents
4. A nickel is 10 cents 5 cents 25 cents	5. A dollar is 50¢ 100¢ 20¢	6. A half dollar is 100¢ 10¢ 50¢
7. $ .05 is 5 cents 50 cents 5 dollars	8. 1¢ is 10 cents 1 cent 1 dollar	9. $5 is 50 cents 5 cents 5 dollars
10. $ .10 is 10 dollars 10 cents 1 dollar	11. 25¢ is 25 cents 25 dollars 10 cents	12. $ .50 is 50 dollars 50 cents 5 cents

Extension

___ married ___ single
___ divorced ___ widowed
___ separated

DIRECTIONS: CIRCLE THE CORRECT ANSWER.

1. How much is it?

It's 95¢.
It's 90¢.
(It's $1.00.)

2. How much is it?

It's $1.50.
It's $1.75.
It's $1.25.

3. How much is it?

It's 36¢.
It's 35¢.
It's 30¢.

4. How much is it?

It's 41¢.
It's 46¢.
It's 56¢.

5. How much is it?

It's $3.90.
It's $3.45.
It's $3.09.

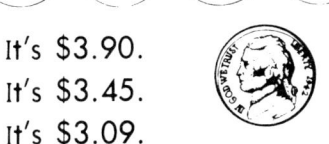

6. How much is it?

It's 50¢.
It's 60¢.
It's 10¢.

7. How much is it?

It's 85¢.
It's 75¢.
It's 80¢.

8. How much is it?

It's $2.25.
It's $2.27.
It's $2.50.

9. How much it?

It's $10.45.
It's $ 5.35.
It's $ 2.50.

Extension

City _____

State _____

DIRECTIONS: CIRCLE THE CORRECT ANSWER.

1. How much is this?

   (It's $8.40.)
   It's $4.35.
   It's $7.30.

2. How much is this?

   It's $10.25.
   It's $15.35.
   It's $ 5.10.

3. How much is this?

   It's $10.21.
   It's $ 5.55.
   It's $ 5.71.

4. How much is this?

   It's $2.73.
   It's $3.00.
   It's $5.70.

5. How much is this?

   It's $4.45.
   It's $1.45.
   It's $1.48.

6. How much is this?

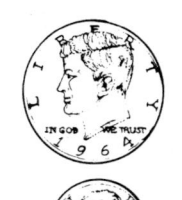

   It's $ 5.55.
   It's $10.55.
   It's $15.10.

Lesson Six, Section II
What's this/that?

MARITAL STATUS
☐ married ☐ single
☐ divorced ☐ widowed
☐ separated

DIRECTIONS: READ.

1. 
A: Is this a cup of tea?
B: Yes, it is.
A: What's that?
B: It's a cup of coffee.

2. 
A: Is this a cup of coffee?
B: Yes, it is.
A: What's that?
B: It's a hot dog.

3. 
A: Is this a doughnut?
B: Yes, it is.
A: What's that?
B: It's a soft drink.

_____
signature

DIRECTIONS: CIRCLE THE CORRECT ANSWER.

1. What's this?

   This is a hot dog.
   This is a doughnut.
   (This is a hamburger.)

   What's that?

   That's a cup of tea.
   That's a soft drink.
   This is a soft drink.

2. What's this?

   This is a cup of coffee.
   This is a cup of tea.
   This is a soft drink.

   What's that?

   That's a hot dog.
   That's a hamburger.
   That's a doughnut.

3. What's this?

   This is a cup of coffee.
   This is a cup of tea.
   This is a soft drink.

   What's that?

   This is a doughnut.
   That's a hamburger.
   That's a doughnut.

145.

date of birth __ - __ - __   age __

4. What's this?   What's that?

It's a map.
It's a mop.
It's a mup.

It's a map.
It's a mop.
It's a mup.

5. What's this?   What's that?

It's a flug.
It's a flag.
It's a flog.

It's a book.
It's a bok.
It's a buuk.

6. What's this?   What's that?

It's a clock.
It's a watch.
It's a clack.

It's a clock.
It's a wach.
It's a watch.

Area Code _____

Zip Code _____

DIRECTIONS: READ AND WRITE.

1.

Is this a hot dog?　　　　　　　　　Is that a chair?

No, _it isn't._　　　　　　　　　　　No, _____

What is it?　　　　　　　　　　　　What is it?

It's a hamburger.　　　　　　　　　_____

2.

Is this a dime?　　　　　　　　　　Is that a bed?

No, _____　　　　　　　No, _____

What is it?　　　　　　　　　　　　What is it?

_____　　　　　　　　　_____

3.

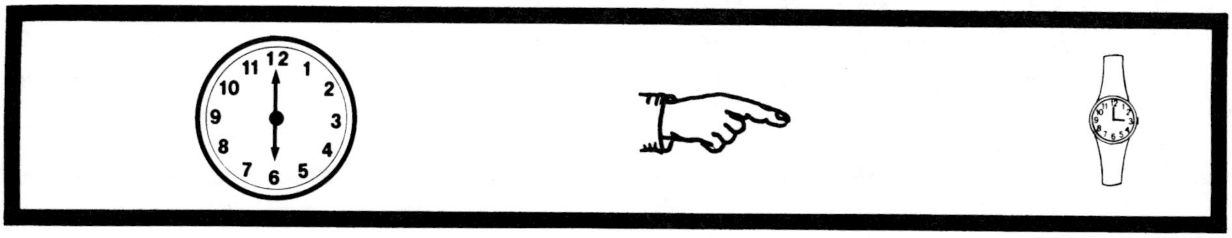

Is this a watch?　　　　　　　　　　Is that a clock?

___ , _____　　　　　　___ , _____

What is it?　　　　　　　　　　　　What is it?

_____　　　　　　　　　_____

147.

_____
place of birth

4.

Is this a window?   Is that a desk?

___, _____   ___, _____

What is it?   What is it?

_____   _____

5.

Is this a flag?   Is that a chalkboard?

_____   _____

What _____ ?   What _____ ?

_____   _____

6.

Is this a half dollar?   Is that a quarter?

_____   _____

_____ ?   _____ ?

_____   _____

148.

Lesson Seven, Section I
It's a/an _____.

Mr.
Mrs. _____   ☐ M
Miss   ☐ F
Ms.

DIRECTIONS: READ.

1.
> A: Is that an orange?
> B: No, it isn't.
>   It's a lemon.
> A: What's this?
> B: It's a banana.
> A: How much are they?
> B: A lemon is 20 cents.
>   A banana is 15 cents.

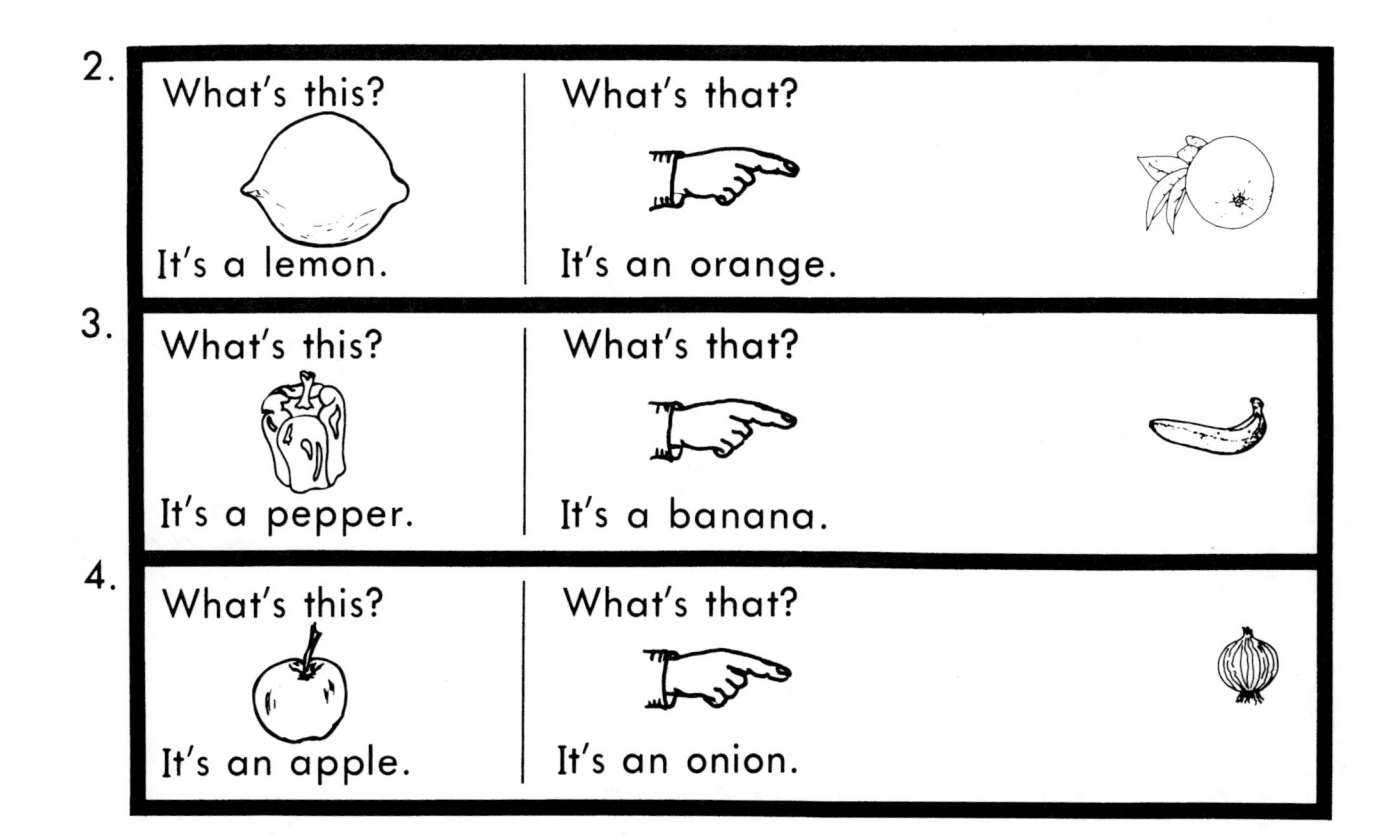

2. What's this? — It's a lemon. | What's that? — It's an orange.

3. What's this? — It's a pepper. | What's that? — It's a banana.

4. What's this? — It's an apple. | What's that? — It's an onion.

Day _____

Time _____

DIRECTIONS: CIRCLE THE CORRECT ANSWER.

1.

What's this?

It's a lemon.
It's an orange.
It's an lemon.

What's that?

It's a lemon.
It's an orange.
It's a orange.

2.

What's this?

It's a pepper.
It's an onion.
It's an pepper.

What's that?

It's an orange.
It's a banana.
It's an banana.

3.

What's this?

It's a apple.
It's a banana.
It's an apple.

What's that?

It's a onion.
It's an onion.
It's a lemon.

150.

Sign here _____

DIRECTIONS: READ.

1.
   A: Is this an onion?
   B: Yes, it is.
   A: Is that an orange?
   B: No, it isn't.
   It's a pepper.

2.
   A: Is this an apple?
   B: No, it isn't.
   It's an orange.
   A: Is that an apple?
   B: Yes, it is.

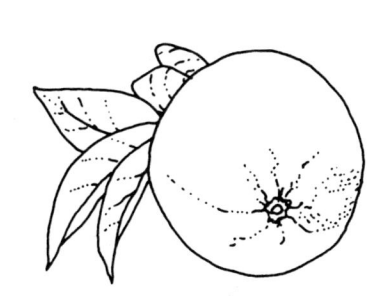

3.
   A: Is this a lemon?
   B: Yes, it is.
   A: Is that an orange?
   B: No, it isn't.
   It's a banana.

151.

DIRECTIONS: READ AND WRITE.

1. Is this an onion?
   ☺ No, it isn't.

   What is it?
   It's a lemon.

2. Is that an orange?

   No, _____

   What is it?
   _____

3. Is this a lemon?

   No, _____

   What is it?
   _____

4. Is that a banana?

   _____

   What _____
   _____

5. Is this an onion?

   _____

   _____
   _____

6. Is that an apple?

   _____

   _____
   _____

152.

Last Name _____

Country _____

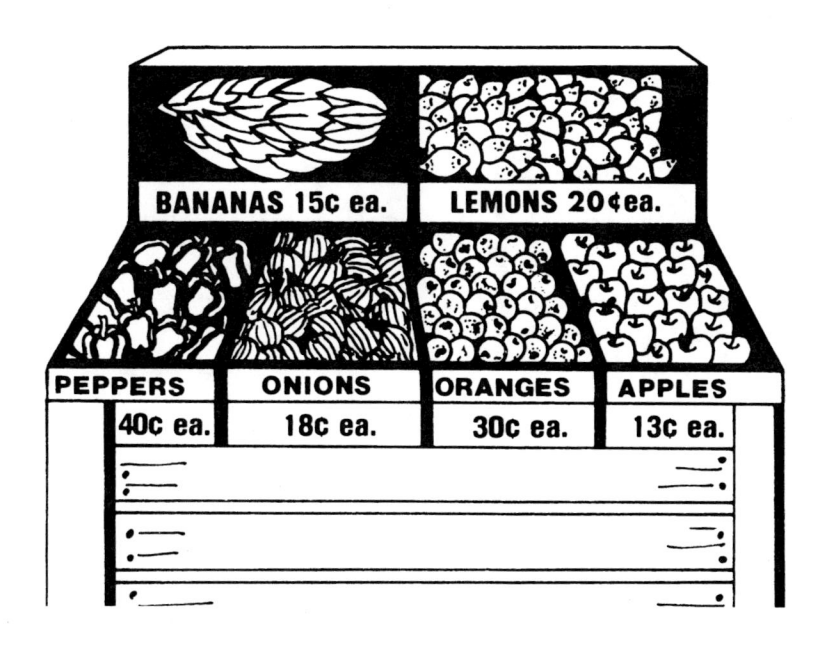

BANANAS 15¢ ea. **LEMONS 20¢ ea.**

PEPPERS	ONIONS	ORANGES	APPLES
40¢ ea.	18¢ ea.	30¢ ea.	13¢ ea.

1. How much is an orange? :)

   It's 30 cents. _____

2. How much is an apple?

   _____

3. How much is a banana?

   _____

4. How much is a lemon?

   _____

5. How much is a pepper?

   _____

6. How much is an onion?

   _____

_____
home phone

DIRECTIONS: READ AND WRITE.

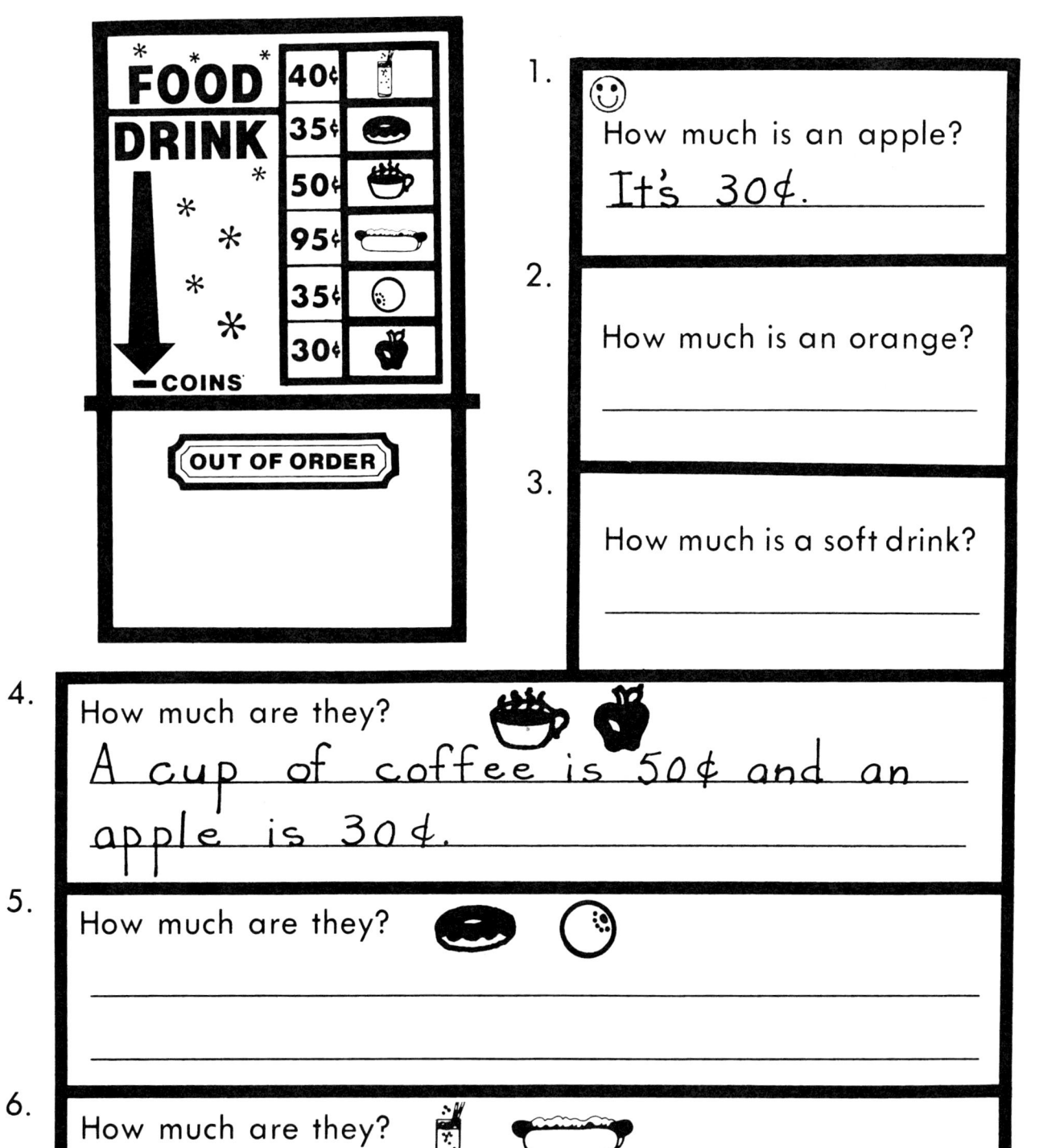

Vending machine:
FOOD DRINK
40¢ — (soft drink)
35¢ — (donut)
50¢ — (coffee)
95¢ — (hot dog)
35¢ — (orange)
30¢ — (apple)
COINS
OUT OF ORDER

1. How much is an apple?
   It's 30¢.

2. How much is an orange?
   _____

3. How much is a soft drink?
   _____

4. How much are they? (coffee, apple)
   A cup of coffee is 50¢ and an apple is 30¢.

5. How much are they? (donut, orange)
   _____
   _____

6. How much are they? (soft drink, hot dog)
   _____
   _____

Lesson Seven, Section II
What are these/those?

birthplace

DIRECTIONS: READ.

1.
A: What are these?
B: These are carrots.
A: What are those?
B: They're cabbages.
A: Give me one, please.

2.
What are these?
These are carrots. 

What are those?  
Those are cabbages.

3.
What are these? 
These are peppers.

What are those?  
Those are oranges.

4.
What are these? 
They're onions.
Give me one, please.

What are those?  
They're lemons.
Give me one, please.

155.

| city | state | zip |

DIRECTIONS: CIRCLE THE CORRECT ANSWER.

1.
   What are these? 

   These are carrot.
   These are carrots.

   What are those?  

   Those are cabbages.
   This is a cabbage.

2.
   What are these? 

   These are lemons.
   This is a lemon.

   What are those?  

   Those are orange.
   Those are oranges.

3.
   What are these? 

   These are cabbages.
   These are cabbage.

   What are those?  

   This is a pepper.
   Those are peppers.

4.
   What are these? 

   These are apples.
   These are apple.

   What are those?  

   This is an onion.
   Those are onions.

Today is _____

DIRECTIONS: READ AND WRITE.

1.

What are these?　　　　　　　What are those?
They're lemons.　　　　　　　_____
How much are they?　　　　　How much are they?
They're 19¢ each.　　　　　　_____

2.

What are these?　　　　　　　What are those?
_____　　　　　　　　_____
How much are they?　　　　　How much are they?
_____　　　　　　　　_____

3.

What _____ ?　　_____
_____　　　　　　　　_____
How _____ ?　　 _____
_____　　　　　　　　_____

157.

Where are you from? _____

DIRECTIONS: READ.

1.
- A: How much are the cabbages?
- B: They're 89¢ each.
- A: Give me one, please.
- B: All right.
- A: Thank you.
- B: You're welcome.

DIRECTIONS: WRITE.

2.
- A: How much are _____
- B: They're _____
- A: Give _____
- B: All right.
- A: _____
- B: _____

Mr.
Mrs. _____
Miss   last   first   middle
Ms.

DIRECTIONS: READ.

1.
A: Are those cabbages?
B: No, they aren't.
   They're carrots.
A: Are these cabbages?
B: Yes, they are.

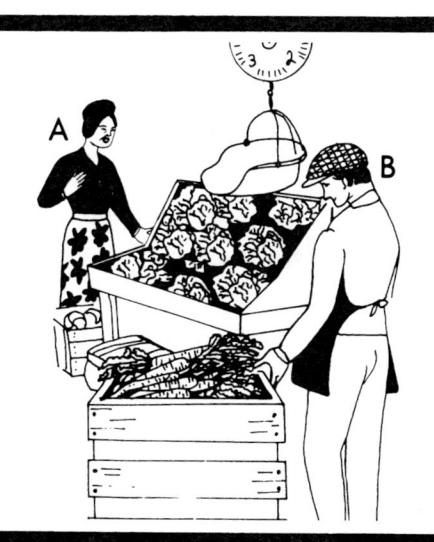

2.
A: Are these lemons?
B: Yes, they are.

A: Are those carrots?
B: No, they aren't.
   They're peppers.

3.
A: Are these apples?
B: No, they aren't.
   They're onions.

A: Are those oranges?
B: Yes, they are.

( ) —

DIRECTIONS: READ AND WRITE.

1.

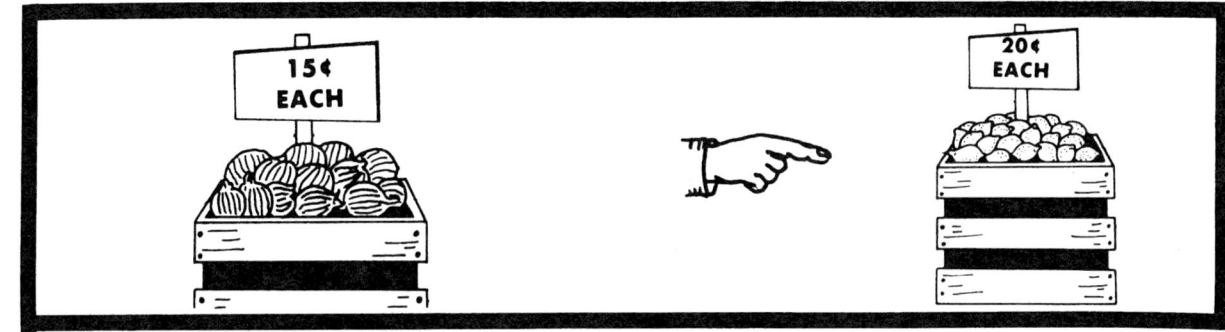

Are these onions?　　　　　　　Are those lemons?

Yes, _____　　　　_____

How much are they?　　　　　　_____

_____　　　　　_____

2.

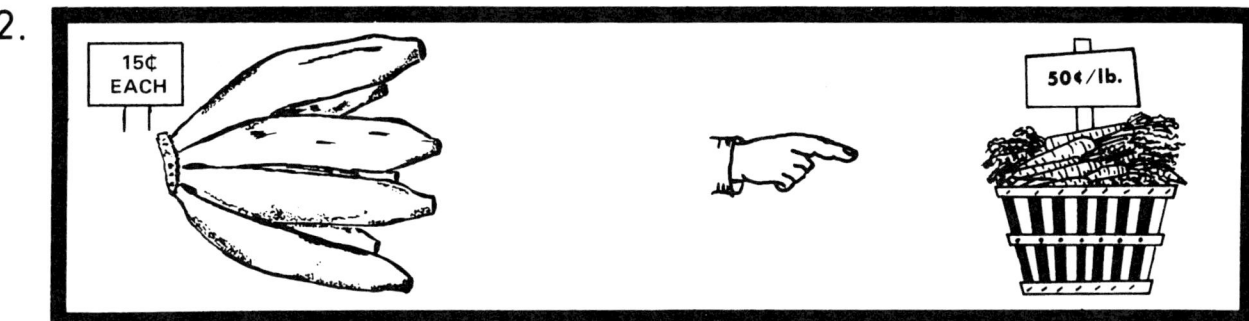

Are these apples?　　　　　　　Are those peppers?

No, _____　　　　_____

What are they?　　　　　　　　What _____

_____　　　　　_____

How much are they?

_____

Odd Man Out

_____
birthdate

DIRECTIONS: PUT AN X ON THE WORD THAT IS DIFFERENT.

| ☺ | Fri. | Sun. | Mon. | ~~It's~~ | Tues. |

1.	nickel	penny	dime	quarter	time
2.	30¢	7:15	50¢	10¢	25¢
3.	hamburger	doughnut	cents	hot dog	soft drink
4.	chalkboard	quarter	nickel	dime	penny
5.	$ .75	$ .25	$ .05	30¢	$ .15
6.	onion	apple drink	cup of coffee	soft drink	cup of tea
7.	Sam	Ann	baker	Ken	Bill
8.	lemon	apple	orange	banana	desk
9.	Please.	market	Thank you.	You're welcome.	Thanks.
10.	cabbages	onions	peppers	apple	carrots
11.	red	Sam	green	brown	black
12.	age	area code	phone	zip code	middle

Sentence Scramble   Sign _____

DIRECTIONS: UNSCRAMBLE.

☺ hamburger.   a   It's
It's a hamburger.

1. are   peppers?   How   much   the
   _____

2. dog?   Is   hot   a   this
   _____

3. cup   That's   a   tea.   of
   _____

4. secretary.   She's   a
   _____

5. is   How   drink?   much   a   soft
   _____

6. one,   me   please.   Give
   _____

7. it?   day   What   is
   _____

8. 25¢   each.   They're
   _____

9. banana   15   A   is   cents.
   _____

162.

Lesson Eight, Section I

He's at the _____ .

It's _____ :

DIRECTIONS: READ.

1. Where is he?

He's at the bank.

2. Where is he?

He's at the barber shop.

3. Where is he?

He's at the post office.

4. Where is she?

She's at the department store.

5. Where is she?

She's at the beauty shop.

6. Where is she?

She's at the laundromat.

7. Where are they?

They're at the airport.

8. Where are they?

They're at the market.

9. Where are they?

They're at the hospital.

date of birth

DIRECTIONS: CIRCLE THE CORRECT ANSWER.

1. Where's Tom?

They're at the market.
She's at the laundromat.
(He's at the laundromat.)

2. Where's Ann?

She's at the bank.
He's at the post office.
He's at the bank.

3. Where are Sam and Ken?

They're at the bank.
They're at the airport.
He's at the airport.

4. Where's Bill?

He's at the department store.
She's at the airport.
She's at the department store.

5. Where are Al and Lucy?

She's at the hospital.
He's at the hospital.
They're at the hospital.

6. Where's Jan?

She's at the bank.
She's at the post office.
She's at the airport.

Age _____ Ht. _____ Wt. _____

DIRECTIONS: READ.

A: Is Tom at the bank?
B: Yes, he is.
A: Is Lucy at the beauty shop?
B: No, she isn't.

DIRECTIONS: MAKE QUESTIONS.

1. He [is] at the airport.
   Is he at the airport?

2. She [is] at the beauty shop.
   _____

3. Jan [is] at the department store.
   _____

4. Ken [is] at the barber shop.
   _____

middle name

DIRECTIONS: READ.

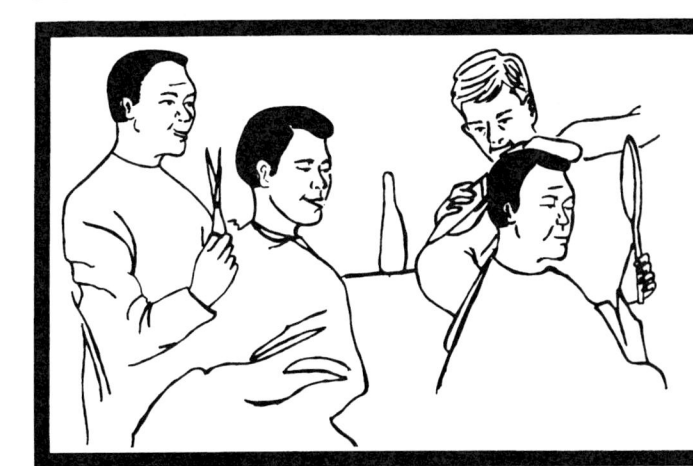

A: Are Sam and Ben at the hospital?
B: No, they aren't.
A: Are they at the barber shop?
B: Yes, they are.

DIRECTIONS: MAKE QUESTIONS.

1. They [are] at the bank.
   Are they at the bank?

2. Ann and Ken [are] at the airport.
   _____

3. Lucy and Al [are] at the market.
   _____

4. They [are] at the post office.
   _____

___ married ___ divorced
___ single   ___ widowed
___ separated

DIRECTIONS: LISTEN AND WRITE.

1.
A: Good morning, Mrs. Lee. What _____ is it?
B: Good morning. _____ 10:45.
A: Is Ben at _____ market?
B: No, he isn't. _____ at the barber _____ .

DIRECTIONS: WRITE.

2. Where's Tom?
He's at the market.

3. _____ Jan?
_____

4. Where are Al and Lucy?
They're _____

167.

Sex M ___
     F ___

5. Is he at the bank?
   _____.

6. _____ market?
   No, _____.

7. _____ ?
   Yes, _____.

8. Are they at the airport?
   _____.

9. _____ ?
   _____.

Lesson Eight, Section II
He's here/there.

_____ - ___ - _____

DIRECTIONS: READ.

1.
A: Excuse me. Where's the barber shop?
B: It's here.
A: Where's the barber?
B: He's there.
A: Thanks.

2.
Where's the spoon?
It's here.

Where's the waiter?
He's there.

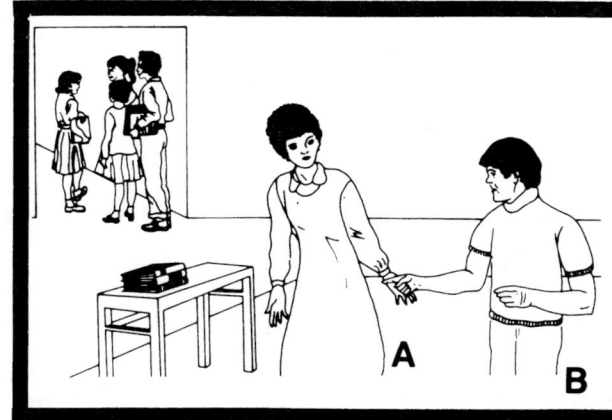

3.
A: Excuse me. Where are the books?
B: They're here.
A: Where are the students?
B: They're there.

4.
Where are the dimes?
They're here.

Where are the nickels?
They're there.

Address _____
no.   street

DIRECTIONS: WRITE.

1. Where's the desk?
It's here.

2. Where's the bed?
_____

3. Where are the books?
_____

4. Where are the lamps?
_____

5. Where's the window?
_____

6. Where are the pens?
_____

7. Where's Tom?
_____

8. Where are the cats?
_____

_____
city   state

DIRECTIONS: READ.

1.
A: Where's the egg?
B: Here it is.
   It's here.

2.
A: Where are the hamburgers?
B: Here they are.
   They're here.

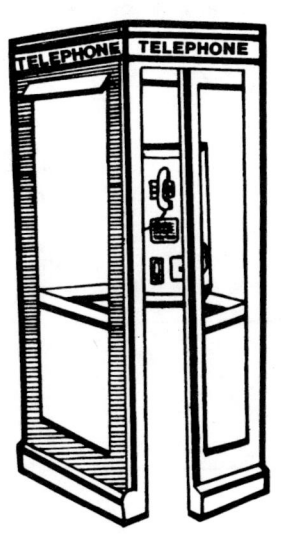

3.
A: Where's the telephone?
B: There it is.
   It's there.

4.
A: Where are the books?
B: There they are.
   They're there.

Today is _____

DIRECTIONS: LISTEN AND WRITE.

1.

Bob and Nan _____ doctors. _____ at the hospital today. Tom is ____ _____ department store. He _____ a salesman. _____ a gardener. Pat _____ at the office. She's _____ a secretary. She's ____ nurse.

DIRECTIONS: LISTEN AND WRITE.

2.

Joe and Jim ____ _____ . They're at the _____ _____ . Al ____ _____ school. He isn't a doctor. _____ ___ student. Mrs. Lee is _____ _____ department _____ . She _____ ____ saleslady.

172.

date

DIRECTIONS: READ.

1. Ken and Tom are gardeners. They grow carrots and peppers. The carrots are here. They're orange. The peppers are there. They're green. Yummy!

2. Mrs. Lee and Linda are cooks. This afternoon, Linda cooks hot dogs and hamburgers and Mrs. Lee makes doughnuts. Ummm, good!

3. It's Saturday. Dad's at the laundromat and Mom's at the market. Tim's at the post office and Jill's at the beauty shop. It's 3:30. How time flies!

country

DIRECTIONS: FIND THE WORD AND WRITE IT IN THE BLANK.

isn't	here	each	It's
secretary	✓doctor	Sunday	market
at	time	hospital	15¢

Bob's a <u>doctor</u> and Jan's a _____. Today, Bob isn't at the _____ and Jan _____ at the office. Today is _____.

Bob and Jan are _____ the _____. The apples are _____ each. The oranges are 20¢ _____. The salesman is _____ and the cashier is there.

_____ 10:30. How _____ flies.

174.

Lesson Nine, Section I
Where are they?

Marital Status ☐ divorced
☐ married   ☐ widowed
☐ single   ☐ separated

A Bedroom

DIRECTIONS: READ.

1. What's this?
   It's a bedroom.

2. What's that?
   It's a dresser.

3. What's this?
   It's a bed.

4. What's that?
   It's a lamp.

5. What's this?
   It's a wallet.

6. What's that?
   It's a purse.

7. What's this?
   It's money.

8. What are those?
   They're glasses.

9. What are these?
   They're pillows.

10. What are those?
    They're shoes.

Ht.	Wt.	hair	eyes

DIRECTIONS: READ.

1. Where's the money? 
It's in the wallet.

2. Where's the lamp? 
It's on the dresser.

3. Where's the purse? 
It's under the table.

4. Where's the bed? 
It's in the bedroom.

5. Where's the wallet? 
It's in the purse.

6. Where are the pillows? 
They're on the bed.

7. Where are the shoes? 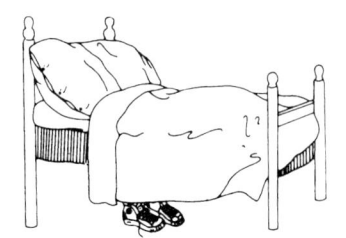
They're under the bed.

8. Where are the glasses? 
They're in the purse.

_____
signature

DIRECTIONS: CIRCLE THE CORRECT ANSWER.

1. Where is it?

The money is [(in) / on / under] the wallet.

2. Where is it?

The cat is [in / on / under] the desk.

3. Where are they?

The glasses are [in / on / under] the dresser.

4. Where are they?

The shoes are [in / on / under] the bed.

5. Where are they?

The pillows are [in / on / under] the bed.

6. Where is she?

She's [in / on / under] the market.

7. Where is he?

He's [in / on / under] the bedroom.

8. Where is he?

He's [in / on / under] the table.

Today is _____

DIRECTIONS: READ.

1.

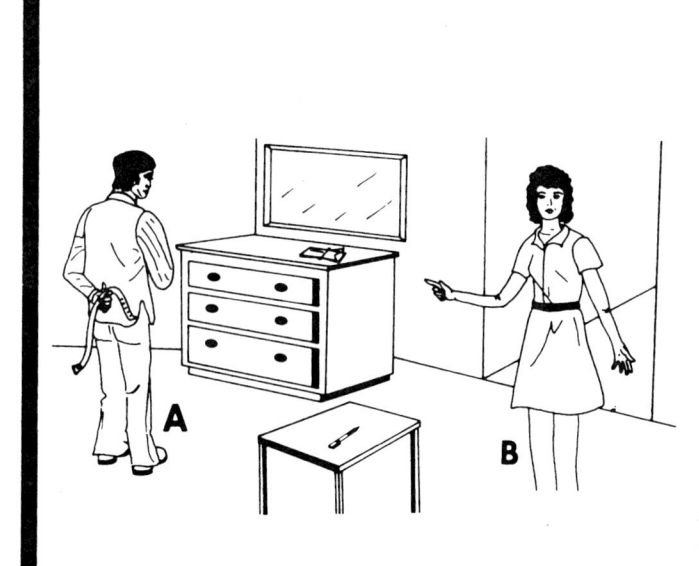

A: _____, I'm late. Where's my wallet?
B: It's on the dresser.
A: Oh, yes. Here it is. Where's my pen?
B: It's on the table.
A: Oh, yes. There it is. Thanks!
B: You're welcome.

2.

A: Excuse me. Where are the cabbages?
B: They're in the box.
A: Oh yes, here they are. Where are the onions?
B: They're under the peppers.
A: Oh yes, there they are. Thanks!
B: It's OK.

DIRECTIONS: CIRCLE THE CORRECT ANSWER.

1. Where's the money?
   There it is.
   (Here it is.)
   There they are.

2. Where are my shoes?
   Here they are.
   There they are.
   There they're.

3. Where's the purse?
   Here it is.
   There it's.
   There it is.

4. Where are my glasses?
   Here it is.
   Here they're.
   Here they are.

5. Where are the windows?
   Here it is.
   Here they are.
   Here they is.

6. Where's the wallet?
   Here it is.
   Here it's.
   Here they are.

7. Where are the pillows?
   There they are.
   There they're.
   There it is.

8. Where is the clock?
   There they are.
   There it is.
   Here it is.

Lesson Nine, Section II
It's a kitchen.

AGE   ☐ 41-50
☐ 15-20   ☐ 51-60
☐ 21-30   ☐ 61-70
☐ 31-40   ☐ 71 and over

① A Kitchen

DIRECTIONS: READ.

1. What's this?
   It's a kitchen.

2. What's that?
   It's a sink.

3. What's that?
   It's a stove.

4. What's that?
   It's a cabinet.

5. What's that?
   It's a counter.

6. What's that?
   It's a refrigerator.

maiden name

WHAT IS IT?

refrigerator   stove   purse
dresser   ✓ lamp   cabinet
wallet   sink   counter
kitchen

1. It's a lamp.

2. _____

3. _____

4. _____

5. _____

6. _____

7. _____

8. _____

9. _____

10. _____

181.

birthdate ___/___/___

DIRECTIONS: READ.

May is a housewife. She's in the kitchen. The hot dogs are on the stove. The carrots are in the refrigerator and the apples are on the counter. The soft drinks are under the sink.

DIRECTIONS: WRITE.

☺ 1. Where's May?
   She's in the kitchen.

2. Are the hot dogs in the refrigerator?
   _____

3. Where are the hot dogs?
   _____

4. Are the carrots in the refrigerator?
   _____

5. Where are the apples?
   _____

6. What's under the sink?
   _____

☐ Mr.
☐ Mrs. _____
☐ Miss   last   first   middle
☐ Ms.

DIRECTIONS: WRITE.

Bob _____ in the _____.

The coffee _____.

The soft drinks _____.

The hamburgers _____.

The doughnuts _____.

Extension

Today is _____

Where do you live?

1. I live in the United States.	2. I live in California.
3. I live in Los Angeles.	4. I live on First Avenue.
5. I live at 6289 West First Avenue.	

Where do you live?

1. I live in _____
2. I live in _____
3. I live in _____
4. I live on _____
5. I live at _____

184.

Lesson Ten, Section I
He's Mr. Lee's son.

name of spouse

The Lee Family

1. 
Ben's the husband.
May's the wife.
They're husband and wife.

2. 
Ben's the father.
Joe's the son.
They're father and son.

3. 
May's the mother.
Linda's the daughter.
They're mother and daughter.

4. 
Linda is the sister.
Joe is the brother.
They're brother and sister.

spouse _____

DIRECTIONS: CIRCLE THE CORRECT ANSWER.

1. Who's he?  
   He's the son.
   He's the wife.
   (He's the husband.)

2. Who's she? 
   She's the wife.
   She's the daughter.
   She's the husband.

3. Who's Joe? 
   He's the father.
   He's the brother.
   He's the sister.

4. Who's Linda? 
   She's the mother.
   She's the daughter.
   She's the sister.

5. Who's Mr. Lee? 
   He's the father.
   He's the son.
   He's the sister.

6. Who's Mrs. Lee? 
   She's the sister.
   She's the daughter.
   She's the mother.

7. Who's Joe. 
   He's the father.
   He's the sister.
   He's the son.

8. Who's Linda? 
   She's the mother.
   She's the daughter.
   She's the brother.

It's _____

DIRECTIONS: READ.

1. A: Good evening, Bob. This is my family. This is my wife, May.
    B: How do you do?
    A: This is Joe. He's my son.
    B: Hi, Joe.
       Is this your daughter?
    A: Yes, her name's Linda.
    B: Hello, Linda.

2. Who's she?
She's Mr. Lee's wife.

3. Who's he?
He's Mrs. Lee's husband.

4. Who's he?
He's Lucy's brother.

5. Who's she?
She's Joe's sister.

6. Who's Linda?
She's Mr. Lee's daughter.

7. Who's Joe?
He's Mrs. Lee's son.

signature _____

DIRECTIONS: READ.

Mrs. Lee is Joe's mother. She's in the garden. Joe and his sister are in the kitchen. The father isn't there. It's Tuesday. He's at work.

DIRECTIONS: READ AND WRITE.

1. Who's Mrs. Lee?

   <u>She's Joe's mother.</u>

2. Where's Mrs. Lee?

   _____

3. Where are Joe and his sister?

   _____

4. Is the father there?

   _____

5. Where is he?

   _____

6. What day is it?

   _____

_____
spouse's name

DIRECTIONS: WHO ARE THEY?

1. He's Linda's brother.

2. _____

3. _____

4. _____

5. _____

6. _____

WHO ARE YOU?

1. _____
2. _____
3. _____
4. _____

DIRECTIONS: WRITE ABOUT YOUR FAMILY.

The _____ Family

My name is _____ . This is my family. _____ is my _____ . _____ is my _____ and _____ is my _____ . _____

_____

_____

_____

_____

Test, Lessons 6-10

last

DIRECTIONS: CIRCLE THE CORRECT ANSWER.

1. Where's the cat?

   It's [in / on / under] the table.

2. Where are they?

   They're in the bank.
   He's in the bank.
   She's in the bank.

3. Where are the shoes?

   They're here.
   They're there.
   Here it is.

4. Are they carrots?

   Yes, it is.
   Yes, they're.
   Yes, they are.

5. Is the banana on the table?

   No, it's on the counter.
   No, it's on the sink.
   No, it's on the cabinet.

6. What is she?

   She's the secretary.
   She's the daughter.
   She's the wife and mother.

7. What are they?

   They're husband and wife.
   They're father and son.
   He's the father.

8. Where's the book?

   It's [in / on / under] the lamp.

191.

Name _____

DIRECTIONS: WRITE THE CORRECT SENTENCE IN THE BLANK.

Here it is.
Are these peppers?
Those are oranges.
The onion is here.
Are those peppers?

They're there.
These are oranges.
✓There it is.
The onion is there.
They're here.

1. Where's the wallet?
There it is.

2.

3.

4. Where are the pillows?

5.

6.
Yes, they are.

7. Where are the hamburgers?

8. Where's the lemon?

9.

10.
Yes, they are.

192.

_____
middle

DIRECTIONS: READ AND WRITE.

1. Where are they?
   _____ airport.

2. How much is it?
   _____

3. Are they bananas?
   _____

4. Who is he?
   _____ brother.

5. Is he at the barber shop?
   _____

6. Are they onions?
   _____

7. What is it?
   _____

8. Who is she?
   _____

_____
       last   first   middle

DIRECTIONS: LISTEN AND WRITE.

1. _____   2. _____   3. _____   4. _____
5. _____
6. _____
7. _____

DIRECTIONS: WRITE.

APPLICATION

☐ Mr. ☐ Mrs.
☐ Miss ☐ Ms.   _____
                  last   first   middle   maiden

_____ _____
  no.   street

_____
  city   state   zip

_____ _____ _____ M _____
 country   birthdate   age   F _____

Marital Status: _____   height _____
                    spouse's name   weight _____
____ married
____ single
____ divorced
____ widowed
____ separated   (___) ___ - _____   _____
                  telephone   soc. sec. number

Time _____   Color of hair _____
Today is _____ Color of eyes _____

              Signature _____

Part 4

Transition to Cursive Writing

Cursive 1: Letters beginning on the line (*ı*)   hair _____

Capital letters

1. *r I I*

2. *r J J*

3. *r S S*

Small letters

4. *r i i*

5. *r r r*

6. *r s s*

7. *r t t*

8. *r u u*

9. *r w w*

Practice.

10. *r Iv*

11. *r Sw*

12. *r Iwr*

Cursive 1: Letters beginning on the line (∂∫)   ___ M
___ F   Age ___

Small letters with a loop

1. *b b*
2. *h h*
3. *k k*
4. *l l*
5. *e e*
6. *f f*

Practice.

7. *fl*
8. *kiss*
9. *he*
10. *she*
11. *it's*
12. *Street*
13. *write*

Cursive 1: Letters beginning on the line (_r_)

age	date of birth

Small letters that go below the line

1. *r j j*
2. *r p p*
3. *r y y*

Practice.

4. *r jet*
5. *r pill*
6. *r yes*
7. *r her*
8. *r ship*
9. *r we're*
10. *r birth*
11. *r they're*
12. *r pepper*
13. *r three*

Cursive 2: Letters beginning above the line with rounded backs (✓ ⌒)

_____
sign

Capital letters

1. ✓ *A A*
2. ✓ *A a*
3. ✓ *C C*
4. ✓ *D D*
5. ✓ *O O*

Practice.

6. ✓ *Albert*
7. ✓ *Church*
8. ✓ *Dress*

Small letters

9. ✓ *a a*
10. ✓ *c c*
11. ✓ *d d*
12. ✓ *o o*

Cursive 2: Letters beginning above the line with rounded backs (a c)

height _____
weight _____

Small letters that go below the line

1. *q q*
2. *q q*

Practice.

3. *gets*
4. *cat*
5. *Age*
6. *Closed*
7. *Dad*
8. *Open*
9. *date*
10. *glass*
11. *desk*
12. *quarter*
13. *apple*

Cursive 3: Capital letters beginning above the line that go straight down (_1_)

country

1. 1 1
2. 1 B B
3. 1 I I
4. 1 J J
5. 1 P P
6. 1 R R

Practice.

7. 1 Bob
8. 1 Barber Shop
9. 1 There
10. 1 Tuesday
11. 1 First
12. 1 Please
13. 1 Post Office

Cursive 4: Small letters beginning on the line that curve to the right (*cr*)

Spouse

1. *r r*
2. *r m*
3. *r n*
4. *r v*
5. *r x*
6. *r z*

Practice.

7. *r name*
8. *r man*
9. *r number*
10. *r very*
11. *r stove*
12. *r exit*
13. *r zip code*

203.

Cursive 5: Capital letters that loop above the line
and round off slightly to the left (*I J*)

maiden name

1. *I J*
2. *I H*
3. *I K*
4. *I N*
5. *I M*
6. *I W*
7. *I Z*
8. *I Z*

Practice.

9. *I Hello*
10. *I No*
11. *I Mexico*
12. *I Ken*
13. *I What's*

204.

Cursive 6: Capital letters beginning above the line that round off to the right on the bottom line (_2_)

birthdate

1. *I*
2. *I X*
3. *I V*
4. *I U*
5. *I Y*

Practice.

6. *I X-ray*
7. *I Van*
8. *I Up*
9. *I Under*
10. *I United States*
11. *I Yes*
12. *I You*
13. *I You're welcome.*

Cursive 7: Capital letters beginning above the line that loop to the right (_ℓ_)

Hair Color

1. _ℓ_
2. _ℓ E_
3. _ℓ L_

Practice.

4. _ℓ Enter_
5. _ℓ East_
6. _ℓ Early_
7. _ℓ Evening_
8. _ℓ Lamp_
9. _ℓ Last_
10. _ℓ Laundromat_
11. _ℓ Lawyer_
12. _ℓ Lemon_
13. _ℓ Lee_

Cursive 8: Capital letters beginning on the line that loop to the left (*ℐ*)

1. ↱ *I*
2. ↱ *J*
3. ↱ *I*

Practice.

4. ↱ *I'm*
5. ↱ *It's*
6. ↱ *Joe*
7. ↱ *Japan*

_____   _____
        (signature)   (sign here)

8. *Sunday*
9. *Monday*
10. *Tuesday*
11. *Wednesday*
12. *Thursday*
13. *Friday*
14. *Saturday*

Writing a Personal Letter

> June 28, 19____
>
> Dear Ann,
>   How are you? I'm fine.
> My address is _____
> _____
> My telephone number is
> (___) ___-_____. Please write
> or call.
>   Yours,
>   _____

DIRECTIONS: WRITE.

Test,
Cursive Writing

_____
signature

DIRECTIONS: MATCH THE CAPITAL LETTER WITH THE SMALL LETTER.

a	x	H	l	F	q
m	j	O	v	L	k
P	p	L	e	C	f
G	d	B	r	W	z
U	a	V	y	X	n
Q	s	I	h	I	c
X	u	R	b	N	w
S	m	E	i	J	t
D	g	Y	o		

DIRECTIONS: WRITE THE ALPHABET.

A a _____ _____ _____ _____
_____ _____ _____ _____ _____
_____ _____ _____ _____ _____
_____ _____ _____ _____ _____
_____ _____ _____ _____ _____
Z z

area code	phone

_____ married _____ divorced
_____ single   _____ widowed
_____ separated

area code	phone

_____ married _____ divorced
_____ single   _____ widowed
_____ separated